If you love eating and entertaining with nothing but the freshest foods, this is the book for you. In Amen to the Garden, Kim shares her love of family, gardening and cooking through her vibrant photography and innovative recipes.

She shows you how to use fresh foods to create "get the party started" dips, wonderful salads, "out of this world" dinner favorites, and so much more! Kim shares her "waste not, want not" philosophy in the garden and in creating a wide range of spectacular foods, juicing and making hot sauce! You'll even learn how to preserve herbs, greens, peppers, and seeds to save for next year's garden.

Amen to the Garden will inspire you to whiz up a smoothie, head outdoors to plant some seeds and pick some dandelions then get busy in the kitchen whipping up fresh delectable dishes to delight your family and friends.

So, come have a seat at the table!

amen to that!

AN ORGANIC GARDEN GIRL COOKBOOK

From my Alexandria home and garden to yours. Enjoy! Kim :)

amen to the garden

DANDELIONS TO DINNER

*Photographs by **Kimberly Cataldo Thompson***

KIM CATALDO THOMPSON

Balboa Press books may be ordered through booksellers or by contacting:

Balboa Press
A Division of Hay House
1663 Liberty Drive
Bloomington, IN 47403
www.balboapress.com
1 (877) 407-4847

ISBN: 978-1-9822-2866-8 (hc)
ISBN: 978-1-9822-1470-8 (e)

Library of Congress Control Number: 2018913149

Printed in China.

BALBOA.
PRESS
A DIVISION OF HAY HOUSE

DEDICATION

This book is dedicated to my amazing kids, Cristina, Calvin and Nolan, now amazing young adults. I'll always believe in you and there is no limit in this world to what you can do. Thank you for your infinite love and patience and for being the best recipe testers ever! Thanks for telling me to write them down – for me, they are written memories of you growing up and you are my inspiration. It has always been, and remains to be my greatest pleasure to cook for you and with you. I love you all to the moon and back and around the sun!

I am grateful to my husband, Roby, who made it possible for me to be a stay-at-home Mom, organic gardener, and do the many things I was able to do for our family.

And to dear Sadie Rose, our precious family toy poodle, thank you for your unconditional love. You could smell my roast chicken and carrots a mile away! I will miss my garden, kitchen, and napping buddy.
May you rest in peace. April 27, 2002 - June 16, 2018.

contents

Mr. Turt

INTRODUCTION

Ever since I was a kid I have relished being outside playing in the dirt, especially making mud pies in the neighborhood with my friends. More time was spent outside than in and from as far back as I can remember, I have always had a love and respect for plants, animals and nature. I loved foraging in the woods behind our house looking for treasures and trying to catch chipmunks. Who knew many years later, chipmunks would be feasting in my garden. My parents always had such a pretty garden. Growing up in an Italian, German and English family, I learned early on to appreciate the love that went into home grown food, cooking for family, and especially, that food brought everyone together.

I grew up with an older sister and a younger brother and we all helped Mom and Dad in some way out in the garden and yard. I was a weeder, and fondly remember those times I was sent out at dinnertime to pick some parsley or a tomato and how I would happily gather hazelnuts in the front yard for my dad. My Italian grandparents and father loved dandelions, and as a child my dad was always sent outside by his parents to pick dandelions for dinner – maybe that's why they are my favorites. Dandelions and their family memories are steeped in my blood.

Sure I helped Mom in the kitchen here and there, mostly on holidays, but it wasn't until I was a freshman in college that I missed her cooking so much, I would call her for recipes. To this day, I will always remember that first meal I cooked up in the basement kitchen of my dorm – my mom's famous rice and pork chops! Cooking that meal felt like being home! I began regularly cooking for friends down in that basement on the weekends and looked forward to it all week.

When home, I was obsessed with watching Julia Child with my parents and then later, Emeril Lagasse, a fellow Bay Stater. There were so many more influences to my cooking, the most being my families'. But long before Food Network, it was chefs like Jacques Pépin, Madeleine Kamman and Nathalie Dupree. I began watching them on public television and collecting their books. I have now been collecting cookbooks for over thirty years!

When I first started cooking in my own kitchen as a newlywed, I had a tiny galley kitchen with my pans hanging on the wall Julia Child style. I LOVED this kitchen and still miss it because I could reach out for whatever I needed at arm's length. I kept pots of herbs on the window sill in the tv room. So, in this wonderful small space, my passion for cooking and gardening became the natural evolution of my life. Julia's books and the *Silver Palate* cookbook became my bibles. Cooking for friends was so fun and I loved bringing dishes into work on party days. I always had writing a cookbook in my head.

Fast forward to three small children and my life as a stay at home mom, making breakfast before school, packing three school lunches a day and making dinner every night, not to mention being the snack lady, or casserole bringer to many a childhood event.

Shuttling busy kids around taught me to be well-prepared and to prep as much as I could with any window of time that I had – even if it was just 10 minutes - I could wash my lettuce for dinner, or place the cupboard ingredients on the counter. I learned to always make some extra to freeze for the days when I knew I wouldn't have time to cook. Frozen pesto always made the fastest pasta meal! Sure we had times when we ordered takeout. These were times I forgot to pull something out of the freezer, didn't have time, or was just plain tired and wanted a break. More often than not, these meals never satisfied us.

As our family grew, so did our garden. We started small with the basic Simon and Garfunkel herbs parsley, sage, rosemary and thyme, plus a few peppers and tomatoes. Every year we expanded the garden, and now 29 years later, we grow about 85-100 varieties of peppers and 60 varieties of tomatoes. The kids all became big helpers and a new generation of garden memories had begun. My daughter helps with seedling transplants, my husband plants all the flowers, and shares with my sons in the hard work of getting the garden ready to plant. I was and still am the "Pepper Queen". From our gardening tradition came one of our favorite family days of the year, when every Mother's Day, we take a trip down the street to our favorite garden nursery where we all look around and each put whatever catches our eye on the wagon. Plus, I always get to pick out a huge ceramic planter for my deck. Then we head home, gather up my many seedlings, and together we plant as much of the garden as we can. My deck is overflowing with beautiful planters!

Me and My Kids

In gardening, sometimes things grow well and sometimes they don't. Sometimes you get lucky with the weather and other times it's too hot or rains too much. Just like gardening surprises, food surprises pop up too. Early in our family life, a personal health scare shifted my cookbook writing course to the study of naturopathy for 17 years, and then on to become a certified integrative nutrition health coach. During that time, four out of five family members discovered they had gluten intolerance. I had yet more learning to do in the kitchen. Having always loved different cuisines, I expanded my basic dishes and jumped head first into Hawaiian, Japanese, Korean, Thai, and Vietnamese foods, among many others. Everywhere we traveled in the world, I added a new cookbook to my collection on the particular cuisine of the places we visited and, of course, whenever possible acquired pepper plant seeds. Like my gardening, my cooking is a continual learning adventure and has evolved and improved year after year.

Time does fly, and I am now heading into my third year as an empty nester with two college graduates and a junior in college. My cookbook collection has now overflowed from my kitchen to my family room and basement, 406 books and counting! Back in 2012, my daughter introduced me to Instagram. Having always photographed my garden and food (albeit not with a phone), it became completely natural for me to post and share what I was growing and what I was whipping up in the kitchen. Who would have thought I would make so many fabulous friends that loved pictures of our garden and wanted to taste my food? In fact, it was the encouragement of many (and you know who you are), that set this book in motion. Yes, it was finally time to begin writing my cookbook.

As a kid from two big families who always cooked for their families, I learned that "homemade is best."

I was taught to "waste not, want not" from my mother, grandmothers, and aunts, which applies to all my cooking. So, I learned to make many great uses from leftovers, like my **striped bass burgers** or **Skuna Bay salmon cakes**.

I also enjoyed grocery shopping with Mom and watched and learned how to pick the best ingredients. I just choose what's crisp and as fresh as I can get, trying to stick with the seasons. Unless I'm making something specific, I just buy what catches my eye and then the recipes usually come as I see what's in the fridge and cupboard. I never buy a tomato when the season is over, so in winter I'll use jarred tomatoes. I always try to get organic and if not, I follow the dirty dozen and clean fifteen list which you can find at the Environmental Working Group (see **resources**). If I plan on making a certain something but can't get the fresh ingredients I want, I change my plan.

I work with a continual rotation of fresh ingredients: what's growing in the garden and what I pick up at the market and have in my cupboard. Sometimes, I'll make a salad dressing to last a few days and I'll make enough of one thing to last 2 days. For example, I'll make a double batch of **jasmine rice** one night and serve it with **our favorite lemongrass beef**, then the next night I'll turn it into my **Chinese style vegetable fried rice** making it a combination by adding any leftover vegetables and beef. I'll make **herby spring risotto with lettuce** so I can make the **arancini di riso** (rice balls). No complaints with any of these dishes! It depends on what I'm in the mood for – and that's really how I roll - in the garden and the kitchen - and from one meal to the next. My family and friends love these recipes and I'm always asked if I will be making my this, or my that, or serving this or that – which tells me I'd better be making it!

My time in the kitchen is a joy. It's my meditation time where love is always the main ingredient – in truth, my three loves: family, cooking and gardening. It is my pleasure to share my recipes and tips with you through the pages of this book. I hope you'll return to them again and again, even creating some of your own. Mostly I hope this book inspires you to plant a seed, eat a weed, play with your food and have a blast in the kitchen!

Love and dandelions,
Kim

Echinacea Flower

ABOUT THE BOOK

A few things to note while enjoying this cookbook:

You will notice interesting titles of dishes because when I create a recipe, it may be named for who requested it, what the celebration was, or whatever was going on that day. On my recipe cards, I sometimes jot down little notes about who was there and even who was not and where they were. Plus, I may even note interesting facts about the weather – maybe there was a blizzard and I whipped up some **crock pot taco meat** I made ahead in case the power went out. So, my recipes are not only memories of the food, but of the day it was made, bringing me back to our togetherness and remembering a meal that brought us all smiles.

When reading my recipes, you may see other bold italicized recipes referred to within them. This means that those recipes are conveniently available to you elsewhere in the book. Simply refer to the index or the contents page of each main section. There are also **notes** after some ingredients which refers to more explanation at the bottom of that page.

In the words of Julia Child, "No one is born a great cook, one learns by doing." I resonate with this quote so much. I remember growing up helping Mom clean up and put away leftover dinner food. I could never gauge the size of the container and always had one way too big for the amount left. So then I'd ask her and, even though what she picked never looked like the food would fit, she always knew exactly the right size! That to me is like cooking because the more you do it, the more natural it becomes.

I've learned to read through the recipes first. That way, you can see what you may want to add or omit to your tastes, and to understand the general instructions. Next, have all the ingredients ready, then you are good to go for each step of a recipe. Experiment with what you love and what appeals to you, leaving out what you don't like. Recipes are ideas and ingredients are versatile – use them as a guide to what's available to you. I don't want you not to make a dish because you're missing an ingredient or two, and I don't want you running out to the grocery store for one ingredient. If my recipe calls for fresh basil and you've got parsley, then use that. If you don't have either, use a pinch of your favorite dried herbs. You'll soon be creating special dishes your family loves. As Thomas Keller said, "A recipe has no soul, you as the cook must bring soul to the recipe."

Some of the recipes take more time than others, so try them out on a weekend and do certain parts earlier in the day so it makes it easier to finish at dinnertime. If you want to make the **chicken parmigiana**, for example, make the breadcrumbs on the weekend and the day you want to make the dish, pound the meat in the morning so you can just get cooking when ready. Or, if you want to make any of the **wedge salads**, make the dressing and wash and split your lettuce early in the day. That makes it a breeze to assemble at dinner. More often than not, if things aren't made ahead, dinner doesn't get made. Being well prepared makes cooking fun and run more smoothly. Believe me, I've had many stressful times in the kitchen when juggling multiple dishes with cook times.

All the recipes in this book may be made gluten free and options are provided in **my cupboard** for ingredients or brands we like the most. Look here for the specific ingredients I like to use. Stocking up on my favorites, especially when on sale, makes it easier to put together last minute meals, like the **open face salmon sandwiches** or the **mackerel salad in avocado boats**. Home-made gluten-free breadcrumb recipe options for any dish requiring breadcrumbs are located in the **miscellaneous** section. Even if I list gluten-free ingredients in any given recipe, the recipe may be made with any of your favorite bread, flours, or pasta.

All olive oil I use is **extra virgin olive oil**, so if it is listed olive oil, it is extra virgin. Unless I am using a specialty salt, which I list, all other salt is listed as **salt mix** and is 3 parts grey sea salt to one part Himalayan pink salt. It is the main seasoning salt I use in my kitchen.

Adding special touches to a meal, such as pretty flowers or herbs, makes everyone feel special and makes food look gorgeous. Please be sure to check wild edibles (see **resources**) in your yard before eating them.

Many times when I cook, I don't measure, so if a recipe says "about 2 spoonfuls," I will also say, about 4 tablespoons if you prefer to measure.

Some of my recipes don't have serving sizes... I cook for a variety of family and friends and sometimes it's hard to say exactly how many people a recipe would serve, so if you come across one with no serving size, take a look at the ingredients to see how much or how little to judge.

Many recipes are used in more than one way, such as the **boursin cheese spread** and **spinach boursin stuffed mushrooms**, so if you'd like to try one recipe utilizing another one, making a double batch will save you time.

Note that many recipes are served and listed together such as the **boursin burgers** and **special sauce**, but you will also find the sauce listed in the index under **sauces**, as well as listed with the burger. The page number(s) of each recipe is also located on the recipe contents list in each section. And since the sauce is served with the **zucchini fries**, it will also be indexed under vegetables and zucchini fries. This way you can find recipes easily if you don't want to make one part of it, but want to make another.

Lastly, a note about the brands referred to in this book. I mention these to you because, in my experience, they are what tastes the absolute best and works for my recipes and our families' tastes. I have received no compensation, in kind or otherwise, from any of these resources as of this publication date. These products are awesome and align with my sense of values. Feel free to experiment and try some out if you wish.

Now, let's get busy in the kitchen!

organicgardengirl

MY CUPBOARD

I am one of those people that always has a backup in case I run out of something. In some instances, I have a backup to my backup! Having raised three super busy kids, keeping a bunch of "extras" in my cupboard was sometimes a huge lifesaver, especially for those snack emergencies or the "I have to bring in brownies tomorrow for the whole class!" This also gives me the freedom to have fun in my kitchen. If I'm in the mood to fix something spur of the moment or try something new, I'm ready! I have several staples and specific brands I use which I share below. I'm sure you have some great stand-bys of your own, feel free to email me and share.

Asian Ingredients
I keep a full pantry of ingredients, so I can make anything I'm craving. I use Red Boat fish sauce, any organic coconut milk and curry pastes by Maesri. For all gluten-free organic condiments, you can't beat Wan Ja Shan for ponzu and Worcestershire sauce, or soy sauce. I also like San -J for organic Tamari. I keep a good stash of Annie Chun's or Thai Kitchen brand rice and bean thread (cellophane) noodles which I use for **Singapore noodle** and **best ever cellophane noodles**. Luckily, my favorite Thai award-winning restaurant has a store right next to it, so I get many ingredients there. If I don't have lemongrass in the garden, I can find it at many grocery stores. I grow many varieties of Asian peppers and get my kaffir lime leaves right off my tree!

Beans and Legumes
Any organic brands such as Whole Foods 365.

Broths and Stocks
I make plenty of my own broths, stocks and bone broths, but there are times when you need it and you find yours frozen. The only brand I use is Imagine brand for all chicken, beef and vegetable stocks.

Bread
Since having gone gluten free, we have tried practically every gluten-free bread under the sun and our favorite is Udi's. They have all sorts of breads, hamburger buns, hot dog buns, bagels, French bread, muffins, pizza crusts etc. This is the only brand I make my breadcrumbs from. We do also like Canyon Bakehouse and Rudi's gluten-free bakery makes the best flour tortillas I use for quesadillas, rollups, enchiladas and more.

Canned Fish
I keep a good stock of a variety of canned and tinned fish. Some brands I love include, Wild Planet, Crown Royal, Cento, Cole's, Oritz, Tonnino, and Royal Red for wild red salmon. I also stock up sometimes by ordering from Vital Choice. See **resources**.

Cheese
I always grate my own cheese as most pre-grated cheeses contain wood pulp to keep them from sticking together. All brands of Italian cheese I use are authentic to their regions. Some cheeses I like raw and I always look for organic. See **note** with **blue cheese dressing** for my favorite blue cheeses.

Condiments

I use any organic ketchup, usually the one with the least amount of sugar. The mayonnaise I use 98 percent of the time is Whole Foods 365 Organic mayonnaise. (So much so that I bring it to Canada for my tartar sauce when we travel there!) Others I have been trying are the Sir Kensington's varieties such as the avocado and sunflower. They also have an eggless mayonnaise. Of course, I use Grey Poupon Dijon mustard among many unique grain mustards. I buy Kelchner's brand of horseradish which is kept in the cold section of my grocery store.

Crackers

See gluten-free ingredients.

Fresh Ingredients

I always have carrots, celery, garlic, ginger, a variety of herbs, red, white and yellow onions (sweet or cipollini in season), leeks, shallots, scallions, and sometimes turmeric. I choose ethically raised and harvested organic grass-fed meats and poultry. For poultry, I love Bell and Evans and a local brand, Aryshire Farm. The pasture raised eggs we buy are Pete and Gerry's and Vital Farms. The turkey tenderloins I love are Koch's brand, because they are trimmed and ready to go. I use only wild caught fish and for the smoked trout, I use Ducktrap River of Maine, found in the cold section where the smoked salmon is found.

Frozen French Fries

I love Alexia brand for their Yukon gold select and their steak fries, but they also have many different varieties of both white potatoes and sweet potatoes.

Gluten-Free Ingredients

The **beer** I use for the fish batter is Red Bridge, but Glutenberg, yellow label is also a good choice.

There are so many gluten-free **crackers** out there, but my favorites for a water cracker are Absolutely Gluten Free Original Crackers. You can't beat them! They have a few flavors and a nice flatbread cracker. Bretons also makes a great cracker and my son loves all Mary's Gone Crackers. My favorite flavor is the Super Seed Seaweed and Black Sesame.

You can't beat Bob's Red Mill for any organic gluten-free **flours** for baking and cooking. I use the 1 to 1 baking flour for many of the recipes in this book, and made note to that within the recipes. The garbanzo and fava flour is also a nice substitute for pan frying fish. They also have great corn flours. I keep all the flours in the refrigerator.

The gluten-free brands of **pasta** we use most is Tinkyáda, however there are some amazing new products out there. My son Calvin loves Banza, but I have yet to cook with that brand. Check your gluten-free sections of most grocery stores. Also see *Asian ingredients*.

Herbs and Spices

Other than the herbs I grow and dry in the yard, my favorite seasonings come from Penzeys, Frontier Co-op, Simply Organic, and Morton & Bassett. These are all non-GMO, and non-irradiated. Frontier Co-op is also non-ETO (ehtylene oxide is a sterilization chemical commonly used in the spice industry.) Morton & Bassett herbs and spices are preservative, salt and gluten free. Frontier Co-op, Simply Organic and Morton & Bassett are certified kosher. For the *Korean Gochugaru chili flakes*, I like Mother in Law's brand which I get at the grocery store.

Mexican Ingredients

What would a cupboard be without Mexican ingredients? I am always sure to get organic corn in anything we eat with corn, specifically because it is non-GMO. We like Garden of Eatin' and Bearitos taco shells, Rudi's tortillas, Eden Organic or Westbrae Natural for organic canned beans, La Morena chipotle chilies in adobo, organic dried beans, salsas, chilies, jarred pickled jalapeños, olives, corn chips, nacho chips and fresh corn tortillas.

Nuts

I keep a variety of nuts fresh in the refrigerator and a variety in the freezer for back up. Not that I have all of them all the time, but the variety I like are brazil nuts, cashews, hazelnuts, macadamia nuts, peanuts, pecans, pine nuts, pistachios, and walnuts.

Olive Oils and other Oils

As noted in **about the book**, anytime you see olive oil listed, it is always extra virgin olive oil. I choose a variety of cold pressed extra virgin olive oils and it is especially important to buy the oil in brown bottles and it should always list the harvest date. See **resources** for information on the Fresh Pressed Olive Oil Club.

I love any oils by La Tourangelle, such as their grapeseed oil and toasted sesame oil, but also buy avocado oil and walnut oil occasionally. You can also find their truffle oil in most grocery stores. There are plenty of great brands for virgin cold pressed coconut oil that are excellent for high heat pan frying. Refined coconut oil has all the same benefits as unrefined, it just will not have that coconut flavor. I use refined oil sometimes when pan frying and I use the unrefined oil in my smoothies. Brands I like are Nutiva, Dr. Bronner's and Spectrum. I use Spectrum refined medium to high heat coconut oil non-stick cooking spray for my baked "fried" foods and for spraying casserole dishes.

Pasta

See gluten-free ingredients.

Peppers

I'm sure you can tell from several recipes in this book that we are fanatics about hot peppers. As well as the many variety of colors and shapes, peppers all have a unique flavor. Some are citrusy and fruity like the Ají amarillo, or smokey like the chipotle and Jamaican hot chocolate habaneros. Habaneros have amazing fragrance and tinny flavor and the Bulgarian Carrot, Pennsylvania Dutch and Carolina reapers are just downright blow your head off! The flavor of a Thai pepper is indescribable, but so delicious chopped fresh and sprinkled on a grilled steak. Of course my fridge is stocked with homemade hot sauces, but other favorites include Franks Red Hot and, of course, Tabasco and any other unique ones we happen to pick up on our travels. See the **resources** page for where to get amarillo paste and sauce for the Peruvian **lomo saltado** .

Rice

Lundberg Family Farms organic California white, short and long grain, basmati, jasmine and sushi rice I pick up at the grocery store. I also love Lotus Foods for organic Heirloom and Fair Trade specialty rice, such as the Carnaroli rice used in my **herby spring risotto with lettuce**, but also Madagascar pink, volcano, and jade pearl. They also have excellent gluten-free ramen noodles. I like to stock up and I keep all rice in the refrigerator.

Salt

I keep a variety of different salts from many regions of the world. Some are flavored, and some are smoked. Some are fine ground and some are course, and many contain essential minerals. Salts add different flavors and are fun to experiment with. As mentioned in **about the book**, I season most recipes with my **salt mix** and keep the blend in an olivewood container by my stove.

Sugars

I love Wholesome brand fair trade organic sugars for all sugars, including coconut palm sugar.

Tahini

The one I like most is Soom sesame premium tahini. It's easy to mix and has excellent flavor.

Tomato Sauce

The brand I have been using for as long as I can remember is Rao's brand and is always what I use unless I have my own homemade. They have many varieties, but our favorites are the marinara sauce, vodka sauce, arrabiata sauce or tomato basil.

Vinegars

I enjoy experimenting with vinegar, not only in dressings, but in making hot sauces, so I like to keep a variety. Aside from the most used apple cider vinegar for anything and distilled wine vinegar for pickling, the others I keep on hand are Champagne, red and white wine, apple balsamic, balsamic, and sherry.

Wine

I love Martini and Rossi Extra Dry Vermouth for cooking. My mom always used this and I keep a bottle handy in my vinegar cabinet for anything that needs wine, unless I state a specific kind in a recipe.

Planting Potatoes

KITCHEN EQUIPMENT

Heavy duty must-haves:

High Speed Blender
I have had a Vita-mix Turbo Blend 4500 for 17 years – it's one of the best investments you can make. I almost wish it would break so I could get a new model!

Juicer
I have a Hurom Juicer and a Breville Juice Fountain Plus which I use 95 percent of the time for my fresh juices and some sauces.

Mortar and Pestle
I have a couple different sizes and love the large one for making pestos and the smaller one for grinding fresh spices and herbs.

Food Processors
Small and large for various tasks, like making dips, dressings and multiple batches of pesto.

Spice Grinders
I keep two – one for grinding dried hot peppers and one for spices.

Everyday essentials:

Baking Sheets
All sizes – including one extra-large 14 1/2" x 20". I love the ones from Sur La Table. They are thick and sturdy and have substantially reduced my use of foil.

Box Grater and Various Microplanes
For zest, cheese or grating nutmeg and other spices.

Broiler Pans
Usually one comes with your oven and they are great for *baked "fried" chicken* or wings.

Cast Iron Skillets
Small and medium sizes come in handy for browning vegetables and peppers for *pan roasted tomatillo sauce*, and I also love my Mexican comal which is a flat griddle type skillet I love for pan frying the tortillas for tostadas.

Colanders
Various sizes, both handheld or with feet for rinsing beans, fruits and vegetables or draining pasta.

Cutting Boards

Wood or bamboo in various sizes. I only use the plastic color-coded ones for raw foods, especially for pounding cutlets. A large carving board with a juice drip groove is also handy for resting grilled meats.

Enameled Cookware

Perfect for soups and are great non-reactive cookware when working with tomatoes or making hot sauce with vinegar.

Funnels

Extra small, small, medium, and large sizes for bottling hot sauce or for any use.

Glass Jars

All different sizes for salad dressings and smoothies and Ball jars for canning and pickling cucumbers or peppers.

Gloves

I buy nitrile exam gloves that are latex and powder free. They come in handy when preparing raw meats and are absolutely essential for handling hot spicy peppers. See **resources**.

Ice Cube Trays

Plastic or silicone – for freezing peppers and herbs.

Knives – My Favorites

Boning knife
Chef's knife
J.A. Henckels knives – various styles for cutting bread or large fruit, and scissors.
Paring knives – I love the Kuhn Rikon in multiple colors (both straight edge and serrated styles), great for seeding peppers and tomatoes.
Shun Japanese knives - sharp as can be! (There's nothing worse than chopping vegetables or trimming or boning meats or fish with a dull knife!) See **resources**.

Measuring Cups and Spoons

All sizes including odd measurements (such as 3 cups or 2 tablespoons). I like stainless steel spoons, as well as cups. I like glass measuring cups in 8 ounce and quart sizes for pouring sauces and stacking bowl measuring cups for dry ingredients, such as flour or rice.

Meat Mallet

Stainless steel with flat side and tenderizer side for pounding meats.

Mesh Strainers

Handheld fine and medium mesh in a few different sizes for hot sauces, soaking and straining rice, etc.

Mixing Bowls
Various sizes – I love glass or stainless steel and enamel bowls for soaking beans or marinating meats. I especially love the huge stainless steel bowls for gathering herbs, peppers and vegetables in the garden.

Non-stick Skillets
Small, medium, and large – I love Scanpans (see **resources**), plus a few small and medium size green pans.

Pie Plates
Various sizes and or, a 3 piece stainless steel dredging set for dipping and breading **zucchini fries** or **chicken parmigiana** or anything needing a dip in egg, flour or breadcrumbs.

Roasting Casseroles and Pans
Key sizes: 5x6, 6x8, 6x9, 7x9 **1/2**, 9x13 and 10x15 **1/2** – I use mostly glass for marinating, roasting vegetables and for baking enchiladas. I also like enamel casseroles in various smaller sizes for baking and serving dips.

Salad Spinner
Small and large for drying herbs, flowers and greens of all kinds.

Saucepans - Stainless Steel with Heavy Bottoms
Small, medium and large – including 10 and 12 quart soup pots.

Spatulas
Various sizes – I can never have enough of these.

Tongs - Stainless Steel
Extra small, small, medium, and large – for various tasks such as flipping the **thick cut potatoes** to outdoor grilling.

Vegetable Peeler
Plus specialty peelers for julienne slicing in place of a spiralizer.

Whisks
Extra small, small, medium, and large.

Wooden and Bamboo Spoons
Various sizes for sautéing and stirring – plus melamine plastic ones for stirring any raw meat.

Mardi Gras – Get the party started!

dips & SPREADS

"How come people don't have dip for dinner; why is it only a snack? Why can't it be a meal, you know?!
I don't understand stuff like that."
David Puddy, Seinfeld Season 6 Episode 23, The Face Painter

I feel exactly the same way – I just love a great dip or spread and enjoy making them for family and
company to get the party started and give everyone something to snack on before a great meal. These
are tried and true favorites that I make time and again.

ANNETTE'S BOURSIN CHEESE SPREAD

*Many years ago, Annette Goldberg, our family friend when I was growing up, made this creamy spread and it has become a staple in our house for entertaining. This is so much more flavorful than the tiny box you get at the grocery store and so easy to make with fresh garden herbs. Over the years, I have used it in many ways beyond a spread. It is always a good idea to make a double batch to enjoy in my **stuffed mushrooms** and **hot peppers** or **boursin burgers.***

INGREDIENTS

1 8-ounce organic cream cheese, room temperature

1/8 cup mayonnaise

1 teaspoon Dijon mustard

1 tablespoon chives, minced

1 tablespoon dill, minced

1 tablespoon basil, chopped

1 garlic clove minced

Add all ingredients to a medium size bowl and mix well or add all ingredients to a small food processor and blend well. No need to specifically measure the herbs: add whatever you like. Place in a pretty serving dish and top with minced chives. This is best made a day ahead or early in the day of serving so flavors have a chance to blend. Let the spread come to room temperature before serving. Enjoy with crackers of your choice, fresh cut vegetables, and of course potato chips!

CHEESE SLAW

When my children were young, I first tried this at their babysitter's bridal shower and I haven't looked back! It is a crowd pleaser and often takes people by surprise when served in cabbage bowls, which is how the slaw was served at the shower. I usually make enough for two bowls and you can bet one is extra spicy. My daughter, Cristina, loves to make this for her friends and sometimes when I'm at the grocery store, if I even see the cheese, it's in my cart!

🚩 INGREDIENTS

1 block gruyère cheese

1 block Jarlsberg cheese

2 hot peppers of your choice, such as jalapeño or serrano, but yellow cayenne is also delicious, seeded and minced

1 bunch scallions, finely chopped, at least 6-8

Mayonnaise to moisten *(I know - you're thinking mayonnaise and cheese - trust me!)*, about 1/2 cup, but it really depends on how much cheese you have

Pinch of salt mix

Freshly ground black pepper

Cut off the rinds of the cheese and shred in the food processor with the shredder blade or use a hand grater. Transfer to a large bowl and add all other ingredients. Stir in the mayonnaise and mix well, adding a little more if necessary. You may take half of the slaw and add to one serving dish and add more hot peppers for those who like it hot to the second serving dish. If you want to get fancy, peel off cabbage leaves (rinse and pat dry) and add the slaw to the cabbage bowls. Serve with your favorite dippers, such as chips, crackers or pita bread.

SPRINGY DIP

Every year in spring, there will be a variety of volunteer greens (those plants that drop seed and come up over and over again), such as mustard or kale that might be flowering and turning to seed. These are the most amazing flavor bites and always fun to incorporate into a nice garden dip, and of course, dandelions are always included. This dip is a beautiful vibrant green - just like new growth in spring!

▌INGREDIENTS

2 cups any mix of garden greens such as mustard green tops and flowers, collard green tops and flowers, baby collard greens, kale, dandelion leaves, lambs quarters, violet leaves and parsley, saving some pretty decorative flowers for garnish

1/2 cup raw organic walnuts, measured loose, not chopped

1/2 avocado, chopped

2-3 tablespoons olive oil

1 garlic clove

2 tablespoons mayonnaise

Juice of 1/2 lemon, about 2 tablespoons, or more, to taste

1/4 teaspoon salt mix

Freshly ground black pepper

Add all ingredients to a food processor and blend well. Taste for seasoning – perhaps adding more lemon juice. Garnish and serve with your favorite chip or cracker.

GREEN OLIVE TAPENADE

We all love olives and I make any combinations of tapenade with whatever I have on hand. It makes an easy last-minute nibble if you keep olives in your cupboard or refrigerator. This tapenade also goes great on an Italian grinder and makes a fine bruschetta topping.

⚑ INGREDIENTS

1 cup Sicilian green olives, also known as Castelvetrano, pitted

8 Kalamata olives, pitted

1 large roasted garlic clove or 1 small fresh clove

2 tablespoons extra virgin olive oil

1/4 cup mixed basil and cilantro

1 teaspoon lemon juice

Freshly ground black pepper

In a small food processor, add the garlic clove and blend. Then add the olives, basil and cilantro and pulse to blend. You want the consistency to be chunky. Use a spatula to turn out into a medium bowl. Add the extra virgin olive oil and lemon juice. Season with the pepper, but no salt as the olives have enough salt. Serve on toasted ciabatta bread rubbed with garlic, toasted slices of baguette or your favorite pita chips or bagel chips.

Note: *To pit an olive, place the olives a few at a time on the cutting board and cover with a paper towel. This keeps any juice from spraying on your shirt. With the side of your chef's knife, lay it flat on the olive and with your palm, firmly push down on the olive. This will crack the flesh and then you can pick out the pit. Some of the greener olives are tough, in which case you can cut around the pit with a paring knife.*

CANNELLINI BEAN DIP
WITH DANDELION AND PARSLEY

Another fun dip to try in spring or summer when dandelions are plentiful, but equally delicious any time of year with parsley. Delightful creamy beans with slight bitter dandelion – awesome!

▌INGREDIENTS

1 14-ounce can cannellini beans, rinsed and drained

1/2 cup lightly packed dandelion leaves, thin ends of stems trimmed

1/4 cup packed parsley stalks (if using only parsley, add 1/2 cup)

1/4 cup extra virgin olive oil

1/4 cup fresh squeezed lemon juice, more or less to taste

2 large garlic cloves, diced

1 serrano pepper, or any hot pepper, seeded and diced

3/4 teaspoon salt mix

Freshly ground black pepper

Blend all ingredients in a food processor until smooth. Taste for seasoning and serve with your favorite crackers, cucumber or zucchini rounds.

Eggplant Blossom

GARDEN BABA GHANOUSH

Other than making my Mom's caponata spread or my brother and sister in law's eggplant parmigiana, this became my favorite way to use up the garden eggplants. Grilling the eggplant with the alder salt adds to the nice smoky flavor. Use any type of eggplant from the garden or local market to make this dip. On this occasion, it was with my black beauty eggplant.

INGREDIENTS

1 medium black beauty eggplant
   sliced 1/4-inch thick,
   lengthwise

1 tablespoon olive oil or
   grapeseed oil

1/3 cup tahini

Lemon juice, tons to taste, about
   3 tablespoons

1 teaspoon smoked paprika

1/3 cup fresh herbs, chopped,
   such as parsley, basil, dill or
   some chives

1 garlic clove

1 jalapeño pepper or any hot
   pepper of choice, halved and
   seeded

Smoked alder salt or salt mix

Freshly ground black pepper

Rub the slices of eggplant with a drizzle of the oil and season with the salt and pepper. Grill slices until lightly browned and softened. Alternately, you may sauté the slices in a large skillet.

In a small cast iron skillet, add a little drizzle of oil, and sauté the garlic clove whole and the pepper halves. Cook, turning occasionally until softened and the garlic is lightly golden. When eggplant slices have cooled a bit, add to the food processor along with the garlic, hot pepper, and all the other ingredients. Blend well, taste for seasoning, and sprinkle with dill. Serve with gluten free matzo crackers or your favorite water crackers.

NOLAN'S ONION DIP

French onion dip was always a weak spot for me and I've never met anyone that didn't love it. This dip was inspired by Emeril Lagasse, and we change it up in a variety of ways over the many years that we've been making it. This one is aptly named for my son who absolutely loves this dip and helps me make it for Super Bowl Sunday, but you can bet it always makes an appearance in summer and any time we get a craving. Now that he is in college, it is a favorite request for when he comes home. Make a day ahead for the best flavor.

INGREDIENTS

2 medium onions, white, yellow, Spanish or sweet, see **note**

Few sprigs thyme

1 Bangalore hot pepper, or any hot pepper, optional

1 medium red onion, finely diced (pinch of salt and pinch of sugar for sautéing)

1/2 cup mayonnaise

1/2 cup sour cream

1/2 tablespoon distilled white vinegar

1/2 teaspoon salt mix

Freshly ground black pepper

Chives or scallion greens for garnish

FOR ROASTING THE ONIONS:

Preheat oven to 425ºF. Peel the rough outer skin from the onions and trim the base so there is no dirt, but the core is neatly trimmed and left intact. Place on a heavy duty foil sheet large enough to enclose and wrap up top and sides. Drizzle olive oil over the onions, and sprinkle a pinch of salt and black pepper on top. Add the thyme sprigs and any hot pepper, if desired. Roast for about an hour and 15 minutes.

While the onions are roasting, in a medium sauté pan, drizzle some olive oil and sauté the diced red onion on medium to medium low heat. Sprinkle on a pinch of salt and a pinch of sugar and continue to sauté. Stir periodically until onions are caramelized and turn a lovely brown color about 20-30 minutes. Set aside when done.

When onions are roasted and cooled, peel one onion and place in a large food processor. Reserve the liquid from the roasted onions. Add the mayonnaise, sour cream, white vinegar, salt and pepper plus 3 spoonfuls of the liquid from roasting the onions, about 2-3 tablespoons. Pulse blend until all is mixed. Add half of the caramelized red onions and pulse blend quickly. Taste for seasoning – you may want to add a little more vinegar or salt.

Using a spatula, scoop dip into a bowl and stir in the remaining red onions, saving a few to sprinkle on top. Place in a serving dish and sprinkle with fresh chopped chives or finely sliced scallion greens and the remaining red onion. This dip is also great with crispy crumbled bacon mixed in. Serve with your favorite ripple potato chips.

Note: Most of the time I roast two onions so I can use one to make my *German potato salad*, but if you aren't making that within the next few days, roast only one onion. I also usually add a head of garlic too because it's nice to have around, see *miscellaneous*.

Chive Flower

MOTHER'S DAY SALMON DIP

Mother's Day at our house is the best! I always get breakfast in bed and so many nice handmade cards. After our trip to the local garden center, we all spend the day planting the garden no matter if windy, chilly, or rainy. After a full day, this dip makes for great snacking while everyone works together to make me a special dinner. But somehow, I just can't seem to stay out of the kitchen! Two of the main things I do with leftover salmon is make this dip or try the **Skuna Bay salmon cakes**. *You can't go wrong with either one.*

▌ INGREDIENTS

2 cups leftover roasted king salmon, or any leftover salmon, such as the Skuna Bay, flake and place in a medium bowl

6 ounces crème fraîche

4 ounces cream cheese, room temperature

1 tablespoon mayonnaise

3 scallions, finely sliced

1/4 cup chives, chopped, plus more for garnish

2 chive flowers if you have them in the yard for garnish

1 tablespoon dill, chopped

1/2 tablespoon of lemon juice and 1 teaspoon zest

Pinch salt mix

Freshly ground black pepper

In a medium bowl, add the crème fraîche, cream cheese, and mayonnaise. Mix well until smooth. Fold in the flaked salmon and all the other ingredients. To make it fancy, line a serving dish with plastic wrap and place the dip inside and smooth the top, then turn over on a serving platter and gently peel off the plastic wrap. Top with a sprinkling of chives and flowers and serve with your favorite cracker, water cracker or ripple potato chips.

HOT OR COLD
SPINACH ARTICHOKE DIP

How to make everyone smile and say, YAY!! Bring out a spinach artichoke dip! This dip really is a "make it the way you like it" type of dip and you can add whatever you're in the mood for. Add different herbs, hot peppers, change up the cheese, serve with or without artichokes, use kale in place of spinach; it's always a crowd pleaser. Great served hot on a cold winter's day or served cold on a hot summer's night!

▌INGREDIENTS

10 ounces frozen spinach, thawed, and squeezed of excess liquid, or frozen kale

1 can artichoke hearts, each gently squeezed to release excess liquid, cut in half

2 large garlic cloves

1/2 cup mayonnaise

1 cup Pecorino Romano cheese, grated

15 leaves fresh basil, chopped

1/2 teaspoon oregano

1 serrano pepper, or any hot pepper of choice, seeded and minced

1/4 teaspoon salt

Freshly ground black pepper

Preheat oven to 350°F. In a food processor, blend the spinach and garlic. Scrape down the sides of the bowl with a spatula and add in the halved artichoke hearts. Pulse blend again until artichoke hearts are chunky. Turn out into a medium bowl and stir in the remaining ingredients. Transfer all to a heatproof serving dish if serving hot, adding a thin layer of extra grated cheese. Bake for 25 minutes until hot and bubbly. Serve with taco chips, pita wedges or your favorite dipper.

Note: Alternately, serve this dip raw and chilled with bagel chips and potato chips. Picture shown served raw.

SPINACH ARTICHOKE DANDELION DIP

This dip is a great way to sneak in some healthful dandelion leaves and it also makes a great side dish alongside your dinner. See **note**.

▌ INGREDIENTS

10 ounces frozen spinach, thawed, and squeezed of excess liquid

1 can artichoke hearts, gently squeezed to release excess liquid, cut in half

1 yellow cayenne pepper, fresh or from the freezer, seeded, optional

1 garlic clove

1/2 cup baby dandelion leaves, chopped, and a few flowers for garnish

3/4 cup shredded emmentaler cheese plus 1/4 cup for the top, or any swiss cheese

1/2 cup mayonnaise

2 tablespoons lemon juice

Pinch salt mix

Freshly ground black pepper

Preheat oven to 350°F. In a food processor, blend the spinach, dandelion leaves, cayenne pepper, and garlic. Scrape down the sides of the bowl with a spatula and add in the halved artichoke hearts. Pulse blend again until artichoke hearts are chunky. Turn out into a medium bowl and stir in the remaining ingredients. Transfer all to a heatproof serving dish, sprinkling the remaining **1/4** cup cheese on top. Bake for 30 minutes until hot and bubbly.

Garnish with a couple of dandelion flowers and serve with your favorite dipper or alongside any meal as a side dish.

Note: See **dandelion tea** for a quick note on the benefits of dandelions.

TOMATO, MANGO, PLUM JAM

*I first tasted tomato jam in a restaurant years ago and thought it was such a fascinating treat. It was presented at the table as you sat down with cheese and crackers. I remember coming home from that meal scouring all my cookbooks so I could try making it. Thank goodness I came across Emeril Lagasse's version in **Farm to Fork**, which has inspired many a tomato jam recipe. This year, I switched it up a bit and love the added mango and plum. This has a nice background spice and the jam pairs well on your charcuterie board with a variety of meats, cheeses and crackers*

▌INGREDIENTS

Makes 3 cups

2 1/2 pounds tomatoes, about 4-6 medium sized, skinned and seeded and cut into chunks, about 4 cups

1 champagne mango, peeled and diced

3 ripe red plums, peeled, seed removed and diced

1 large lemon, peeled, seeded and flesh cut from the pith (be sure to collect the juice)

8 tabasco peppers, seeded

1 cup fine organic sugar

In a nonreactive saucepan, add all ingredients (totals 4 cups) except the sugar and on medium heat, bring to a medium to medium low simmer. Add the sugar, stirring often and skimming the foam as it comes up, mostly in the first 15 minutes. Continue breaking up pieces of the fruits with the back of a wooden spoon. Don't worry if you weren't able to get all the skin off the tomatoes, by the 20 minute mark, you will see pieces curled up and you can just pick them out with tongs.

At this point, feel free to use an immersion blender to lightly break bigger chunks if necessary, being careful as the mixture is extremely hot. Don't blend completely smooth, just break up the larger chunks.

Make sure your jars of choice are sterilized and hot.

Turn down the heat a notch or two as the jam starts to thicken, stirring often. Remove from heat when thickened at the 30 minute mark. In the hot jars, gently ladle in the hot jam. Twist the tops until closed and just snug. Let them cool on the counter and then store in the fridge.

SMOKED TROUT SPREAD

If you need to bring something to a cocktail party, this is an easy and delicious make ahead hors d'oeuvre. Sometimes I just make it to keep around for a snack.

▉ INGREDIENTS

DAY BEFORE:

1/2 cup sour cream

4 ounces cream cheese, softened to room temperature

4 scallions cut in half lengthwise and then thinly sliced crosswise

Pinch salt mix

Freshly ground black pepper

DAY OF:

2 fillets (8 ounces) smoked trout (Ducktrap River of Maine), skin removed and fish flaked into a medium bowl

2 tablespoons or thereabouts chopped chives and chive flowers for the garnish

1 tablespoon or thereabouts chopped basil

1 tablespoon or thereabouts chopped dill

1 tablespoon lemon juice

In a small bowl with a fork, blend the cream cheese with the sour cream or alternately, blend in a small food processor and then turn into a small bowl. Stir in the scallions, salt and pepper and set aside until the next step is done or can be made a day ahead at this point and kept in the fridge.

In a medium bowl, add the flaked fish and as you go along, remove any small pin bones as you see them. Trout has very small bones, so don't worry about getting them all out. You will see the larger ones and those are the ones you want to remove. This step may also be done ahead. When ready to put everything together, add about 1/2 – 3/4 of the sour cream mixture, the chives, basil, dill, or any combination of your favorite herbs, and lemon juice. If it needs more of the sour cream mixture, add it in, but I find about 3/4 to be enough (the rest is the cooks treat to nibble on).

Taste for seasoning. Turn into your serving dish and sprinkle with chives and garnish with a couple flowers. Serve with sliced toasted baguette slices or your favorite crackers.

Big Bird

salads & DRESSINGS

When my daughter Cristina lived at home, she was and still is the best salad maker, and it was so nice having that help while I prepared the rest of the meal. Now that she's on her own, I had to become salad girl. My deal about salads was that I always had way too many greens for two to three people, so over the years, I have become "wedge" woman, because I find it easier to portion per person. Here you will find all kinds of salads. They make for a great lunch, dinner or side dish.

ITALIAN GIARDINIERA

Giardiniera is a crisp and crunchy combination of fresh vegetables that have been pickled with salt brine, vinegar, and oil. In Italy, giardiniera may be part of the antipasti platter, served as an appetizer before the meal, and served alongside other varieties of vegetables such as artichokes, marinated eggplant and mushrooms, as well as an assortment of cheeses, cured meats, olives, and stuffed peppers of course! I love making this when the garden is bursting with a rainbow of colorful hot and bell peppers. It's fun to prepare knowing you'll be enjoying it throughout winter. Try a dollop of this salad on your favorite Italian cold cut sandwich or organic hot dog!

🔖 **INGREDIENTS**

DAY 1:

1/3 cup diamond crystal or other kosher salt

1 1/4 cups carrots, small dice

4 cups cauliflower (one small head), small dice

2 cups celery, small dice 1/4 inch (about 5 inner stalks)

2 cups fennel, small dice 1/4 inch, one large bulb

1/2 cup garden yellow bell pepper, small dice (or any color-red or orange)

2 garlic cloves, minced

1 tablespoon dried garden oregano

1/2 teaspoon freshly ground black pepper

HOT PEPPER MIX FROM GARDEN:

It looks pretty to dice some and slice others – makes just over 1 cup. Use any variety of hot peppers you like. It could be all one type as well, such as all serrano, or all jalapeño. I just like the colors, as well as the different heat levels.

▌INGREDIENTS

3 serrano peppers

3 hot cherry red peppers

3 spicy Hungarian peppers

3 yellow cayenne peppers

In large ceramic (non-reactive bowl), add ingredients as you chop them. When all of the ingredients have been added, toss lightly and sprinkle salt on top. Pour over enough filtered water to cover. Cover with plastic wrap and refrigerate for a full 24-32 hours.

DAY 2 OR 3 DEPENDING ON LENGTH OF SOAK:

Rinse in batches and drain well. Into another large non-reactive bowl, add the following:

▌INGREDIENTS

3/4-1 teaspoon homemade ground garden hot red pepper flakes or any organic brand hot red pepper flakes

1/2 teaspoon celery seed

1 tablespoon dried golden oregano or any oregano

1/2 teaspoon cracked black pepper

1 cup white wine vinegar

1 cup extra virgin olive oil

1 1/2 cups grapeseed oil

Mix together well and add to the well-drained vegetables. Stir gently and spoon into sterilized jars as big or small as you like, just allowing enough head space to completely cover with oil. Makes about 5-6 pints. When all jars are evenly filled, top off with more oil to cover. Seal and keep refrigerated. Let sit a few days before opening.

GARDEN GREENS SALAD WITH THYME CHIVE DRESSING

The thyme in our garden almost always survives winter and come spring, it is so fresh and delicious that I love using it in dressings and marinades, but feel free to substitute any herbs you have on hand. The dandelion leaves are a bitter and the mustard greens a bit spicy, so the honey and grapes add a nice sweet note.

Serves 4-5

▌INGREDIENTS

2 heads spotted Aleppo lettuce or any bibb lettuce

Couple small bunches volunteer green leaf lettuce or half a head green leaf lettuce

4-6 dandelion leaves

3-4 mustard greens with yellow flowers for the top

Handful of chives, chopped with flowers for the top

10-12 red grapes

FOR THE DRESSING
▌INGREDIENTS

4 tablespoons apple cider vinegar

6 tablespoons extra virgin olive oil

2 tablespoons lemon juice

1 tablespoon local raw honey

1 tablespoon minced garden creeping thyme or any thyme

1 tablespoon chopped chives

1/4 teaspoon Utah sea salt or salt mix

Freshly ground black pepper

Wash the greens and spin dry. Tear or chop the greens and place in a medium salad bowl. Add all dressing ingredients into a jar and shake well. Taste for seasoning and refrigerate until ready to use. When ready to toss, add a handful red grapes and sprinkle with the mustard and chive flowers. This dressing is also nice on an Italian grinder!

ROMAINE WEDGE WITH LEMON THYME VINAIGRETTE

*This salad is as simple as it gets but oh so delicious! My son Calvin loves the light dressing and it makes a nice meal served with the **chicken parmigiana**.*

Serves 2 with enough dressing for 4-5 wedges

🔖 INGREDIENTS

1 large head of romaine lettuce split into a wedge (see **note**)

4 slices salami

Lemon wedges

Parmigiano-Reggiano cheese

Wash and dry the romaine wedges and set each on a plate, or keep in the fridge until serving time. In a large non-stick skillet set to just under medium heat, add the salami slices to render the fat and crisp up, about 5-7 minutes turning occasionally. Lay on paper towels until ready to plate the salad.

LEMON THYME VINAIGRETTE

🔖 INGREDIENTS

1/4 cup fresh lemon juice

1/2 cup olive oil

1 teaspoon Dijon mustard (I don't measure, just use a small dollop, about 1-1/2 teaspoons.)

1 small garlic clove, minced, optional

1 tablespoon minced garden creeping thyme (try basil later in the season)

1 teaspoon local raw honey

1/4 teaspoon salt mix

Freshly ground black pepper

Add all the ingredients to a jar and shake well. Taste for seasoning and store in the fridge until ready to use. When ready to serve, top the romaine wedge with as much dressing as you like. Crumble two salami slices per wedge and grate some cheese over the top. Top with freshly ground black pepper and garnish with a lemon wedge on the side and it's ready to serve.

Note: *To prepare the romaine wedge, trim the core to clean up and then cut a one inch slice lengthwise through the core. With both hands, gently hold the core and pull the lettuce into two wedges. Rinse thoroughly and dry on a clean kitchen towel. I usually do this earlier in the day of serving and keep wrapped in the towel placed in a green bag in the fridge. That way the wedge stays cold and crisp come serving time. Also feel free to substitute a wedge of any of your favorite lettuce for this or any of the wedge salads in this book, such as iceberg, Boston, bibb, or red or green leaf lettuce.*

STEAK SALAD
WITH BLUE CHEESE DRESSING
TOPPED WITH BAKED ONION RINGS

This makes such a great all-in-one meal. If serving with the onion rings, give yourself about 45 minutes before starting the steak, but while the onion rings soak and cook for the first 10 minutes, begin prepping the salad ingredients and dressing.

Serves 3-4

🏷 INGREDIENTS

2 1/2 romaine heads lettuce sliced crosswise, washed and spun dry

2 purple carrots diced or sliced

2-3 multi colored radishes sliced

Handful of dill chopped

4 thin ribeye steaks trimmed of fat or cube steaks seasoned with salt, pepper, and garlic powder

Drizzle of olive oil

In a cast iron skillet, on medium heat, drizzle in the olive oil and pan fry the steaks, flipping once until pink in the center or feel free to grill them. Remove to a platter and let them rest for five minutes before slicing one to one and a half per salad.

Place the greens on individual plates, then sprinkle on the radishes and carrots. Arrange the steak throughout the salad. Drizzle with the blue cheese dressing and sprinkle on the dill and black pepper. Top with the baked onion rings.

BLUE CHEESE DRESSING
🏷 INGREDIENTS

1/2 cup mayonnaise

1/4 cup sour cream, crème fraîche or Greek yogurt

1 wedge (about 0.45 ounces) Roth Buttermilk Blue Cheese, cut evenly in half, reserve one half for extra cheese to crumble on top), or (about 0.26 ounces) Bongrain St. Agur Blue, see *note*

1 1/2 tablespoons lemon juice

1 tablespoon red wine vinegar or 1/2 tablespoon apple cider vinegar and 1/2 tablespoon red wine vinegar

1 garlic clove, chopped

Lots of freshly ground black pepper

1/2 teaspoon my *vinegar red hot sauce* or any of your favorite vinegar based hot sauce

In a small food processor, add all the ingredients except the cheese. Blend well. Then, crumble in **1/2** of the wedge and pulse blend well. Add in the remaining cheese and pulse blend again, but leave some chunks. Taste for seasoning adding a little more vinegar or lemon juice if necessary. The dressing should have a nice tang to it. Make ahead and taste again before serving. Serve extra dressing on the side.

BAKED ONION RINGS

These rings are great with just about anything, but make a nice crispy bite on top of the steak salad.

◼ INGREDIENTS

2 cups buttermilk, or see recipe

1 large red onion sliced 3/4 -inch thick, separated into rings (reserving the smaller middle pieces for something else)

FOR THE COATING:

◼ INGREDIENTS

2 cups gluten free flour, Bob's Red mill 1 to 1 baking flour

1/4 teaspoon my dried red pepper or any dried pepper

1/4 teaspoon smoked paprika

1/4 teaspoon chipotle chili powder

1/4 teaspoon garlic powder

1 tablespoon salt mix

Lots of freshly ground black pepper

Note: I also love Point Reyes, Saga Blue, Danish Blue, Gorgonzola Dolce Igor and Borough Stilton Market Blue Cheeses at about the same weight in ounces as the Roth buttermilk. Many times I find the dressing just right without added crumbles, but if you like them, keep a small portion on the side. I also make this dressing using a smaller wedge of cheese for the Bongrain St. Agur blue because it is stronger flavored.

Place in large glass baking dish or large bowl. Soak slices about 30 minutes, turning occasionally if not totally covered in the buttermilk.

Preheat oven to 450°F. In a pie plate or deep dish, add all ingredients and mix well. Lightly oil a baking sheet. Dip each onion ring into the flour mixture shaking off the excess rub both sides in the oil and place on the baking sheet. When all are done, lightly spray with cooking spray, especially on dry places. Place in the oven on the middle rack. Bake 10 minutes, flip each one using tongs and bake another 10 minutes. Serve on top of the salad or with a nice grilled steak.

CAESAR SALAD WEDGE

This salad looks gorgeous on the plate. We are total Caesar fanatics, so you will notice my Caesar dressings are similar, but are not all the same.

INGREDIENTS

1/2 head romaine lettuce per person

1 prosciutto slice per wedge

3 anchovies per wedge if you like them

Freshly grated Parmigiano-Reggiano cheese, fine grate

Parsley, chopped for garnish

Freshly ground black pepper

FOR THE DRESSING

INGREDIENTS

1/4 cup Sir Kensington's Avocado mayonnaise, no measuring required

1/2 cup extra virgin olive oil

1 tin can anchovies (minus 3 per one wedge – If more than one person likes the whole anchovies to top off their salad, you may need to open another tin)

3 garlic cloves

Juice of 1 lemon

1 tablespoon Dijon mustard, no measuring required

Lots of freshly ground black pepper

In a small food processor, add all ingredients except the olive oil and blend well. With machine running, drizzle **1/4** cup of the oil through the top, and then do the same with the other **1/4** cup. Taste for lemon juice, but rarely needs any salt, especially with the Parmigiano and prosciutto on top.

To plate the salad, place a wedge on the serving plate. Twist a piece of prosciutto and place lengthwise down the center of the wedge. Drape 3 anchovies crosswise on the wedge. Drizzle with the dressing, a sprinkling of fresh parsley and a grating of Parmigiano-Reggiano cheese. Serve extra dressing on the side.

CAPRESE SALAD TWO WAYS

Caprese salads are so simple and satisfying, plus they make one of the easiest side dishes to put together for a summer meal. Just be sure to use the most gorgeous garden ripe or farmers market tomatoes.

CAPRESE SALAD WITH BURRATA CHEESE

Everyone loves a fresh Caprese salad and any leftovers, should there be any, make great additions to BLT sandwiches.

▌INGREDIENTS

4 slices carbon tomato, seeds removed, skinned if you feel like it

4 slices Nebraska wedding tomato, seeds removed

4 slices purple Cherokee tomato, seeds removed

1 ball fresh burrata cheese sliced

Genovese basil leaves

Drizzle your best extra virgin olive oil

Pink flake salt

Freshly ground black pepper

On a small platter, arrange tomato slices alternating colors, tucking in the burrata slices and basil leaves. Drizzle with the olive oil and sprinkle with salt and pepper.

CAPRESE SALAD WITH TRUFFLE BURRATA CHEESE AND PROSCIUTTO

The prosciutto adds a nice bite of salty flavor paired with the sweet juicy tomatoes and creamy cheese. Heavenly!

INGREDIENTS

2 large garden ripe tomatoes sliced, seeds removed, skinned if you feel like it

1 ball fresh truffle burrata cheese

Handful of cherry or grape tomatoes

1 pack prosciutto di Parma slices (about 10)

Genovese basil leaves

Drizzle of your best extra virgin olive oil

Grey sea salt

Freshly ground black pepper

Slice tomatoes into half inch thick slices, removing seeds if desired. Arrange on a serving platter. Twist each prosciutto slice and arrange at one end of the platter. Cut the burrata cheese in half and tuck into two spots on the platter. Tuck and arrange the cherry tomatoes in and around the tomatoes and prosciutto. Drizzle the olive oil all around and slice the basil or tear into pieces and sprinkle around the platter. Season with a pinch of salt and freshly ground black pepper. No need to salt the prosciutto. Add a few basil tops and serve.

PAN SEARED WEDGE SALAD WITH SPICY JALAPEÑO BASIL RANCH DRESSING

I came up with this dressing for my daughter, Cristina, since she isn't a big fan of blue cheese. It also makes a great dip for a vegetable platter.

Serves 2 with enough dressing for 6

INGREDIENTS

1 head romaine lettuce, split in half into 2 wedges, washed and patted dry

2 teaspoons extra virgin olive oil

1 tomato, seeded and chopped

4 slices smoked Niman Ranch bacon cut into lardons (crosswise slices) and 2 more cut in half if making a couple stuffed peppers

1/2 small red onion, thinly sliced

4-6 basil leaves for garnish

In a medium skillet, cook the bacon until crisp, then remove with a slotted spoon onto paper towels to drain. Drain most of the bacon fat out of the skillet, leaving just a remnant. Drizzle about 1 teaspoon of olive oil per wedge and with your hands, rub in and between the leaves. Pan sear the romaine on medium heat in the same pan as you cooked the bacon, about 2 minutes per side. Pan sear the back side first and then the cut side second (feel free to grill if you have that going).

Place each wedge on a plate, drizzle dressing over the top, serving extra dressing on the side. Sprinkle with the tomato, bacon and onion slices. Garnish with chopped basil and freshly ground black pepper. I happened to have some leftover **boursin cheese spread**, so I went ahead and stuffed a couple peppers to serve alongside. See recipe if desired.

SPICY JALAPEÑO BASIL RANCH DRESSING
Makes enough for 6 wedges

INGREDIENTS

1 cup **homemade buttermilk**, or any buttermilk

1/4 cup mayonnaise

1/4 cup Greek yogurt, or 1/2 cup Greek yogurt and no mayonnaise

1/4 cup packed Genovese basil

1 tablespoon dill, chopped

1 jalapeño, seeded and chopped

1 good size scallion, chopped

1 extra large garlic clove or 2 smaller ones

Scant 1 teaspoon Dijon mustard

1/4 teaspoon lemon zest

1/2 teaspoon salt mix

Freshly ground black pepper

Add all ingredients into a small food processor and blend well. Taste for seasoning and store in the fridge until ready to serve.

MACKEREL SALAD STUFFED IN AVOCADO AND BELL PEPPER BOWLS

It has been quite an adjustment over the past three years having become the dreaded empty nester, especially trying to scale back my cooking for 5, which usually meant cooking for 8-10, because I always had leftovers. I love the ease of canned fish, such as mackerel, sardines and tuna. When my husband's out at a game, this makes a quick lunch or easy dinner for one.

▌ INGREDIENTS

1 can mackerel, skinless and boneless in olive oil

1/4 cup red onion, diced

1 celery stalk, diced

1/2 Hungarian Peter pepper, minced

3 tablespoons mayonnaise

2 teaspoons Dijon mustard

1 tablespoon thyme, chopped

1-2 tablespoons lemon juice

Pinch of salt

Freshly ground black pepper

1/2 an avocado

1/2 yellow bell pepper, or any color, seeded

Mix all ingredients except the avocado and yellow bell pepper in a medium bowl. Mound salad in each avocado and pepper "bowl" and serve with extra lemon juice and a side of potato chips. Easily doubled and tripled.

ICEBERG WEDGE SALAD WITH BUFFALO CHICKEN TENDERS AND FETA DRESSING

One day, I started out making my chicken tenders but was craving a wedge salad, so I decided to put the two together and it was a big hit. If making this with the chicken tenders, begin with that recipe first to judge your timing from making to serving.

Serves 4

▌ INGREDIENTS

1 head iceberg lettuce cut into 4 wedges and each wedge cut into 2 smaller wedges

1 red onion, sliced

8 slices Niman Ranch bacon cut into lardons (crosswise slices), browned and drained

Handful cilantro, chopped

1 recipe **buffalo chicken tenders** See **photo** on page 105.

Place two wedges per person on each plate. Sprinkle with sliced red onions, the bacon and cilantro. Place two to three chicken tenders per plate and drizzle with the feta dressing and freshly ground black pepper. The garden cilantro in this was amazing and so much more flavorful than store bought, but use any herbs you like.

FETA CHEESE DRESSING

This dressing was a happy accident as I went to make my blue cheese dressing and found I didn't have any, I substituted my feta and it was a winner. Even if you don't make the salad, but you make the chicken tenders, this dressing makes a fab dipping sauce for them. Need I say more?!

▌ INGREDIENTS

1/2 cup mayonnaise

1/3 cup sour cream

1 1/2 tablespoons lemon juice

1 tablespoon red wine vinegar

1 garlic clove

3/4 cup crumbled Bulgarian feta, loose, not packed (works equally well with French double cream feta)

Freshly ground black pepper

In small food processor, blend all but the feta. Scrape down the sides of the bowl and then add the feta pulse blending just to mix. No need to salt as the feta is quite salty. Turn out into a glass jar and keep in the fridge until serving.

WATERMELON TOMATO ARUGULA SALAD

I've seen many variations of this salad over the years, most not with tomatoes, but there's a reason it's still around – it is an excellent refreshing salad, plus the bonus, it feeds a crowd! Feel free to change it up with different herbs and lettuce. It also makes a great portable salad to take to any picnic.

▌ INGREDIENTS

1 small round watermelon cut into 1-2 inch cubes, fill a large bowl with this

1-2 heirloom tomatoes, seeded and cut into chunks

1 medium 6" cucumber, seeds scooped out or one long cucumber cut in half

1-5 ounce package baby arugula (watercress is also great)

Handful of mint and a handful of basil, about 1 cup total, roughly chopped or torn

15-20 pitted Kalamata olives

4 ounces Bulgarian feta, crumbled

FOR THE DRESSING
▌ INGREDIENTS

2 1/2 tablespoons your best extra virgin olive oil

2 tablespoons lemon juice, or lime juice

1/2 teaspoon dried oregano

1/4 teaspoon fine grey salt

Freshly ground black pepper

In a very large serving bowl that is larger wide than deep, spread the arugula around the bottom. Add the cubes of watermelon, tomatoes and cucumbers. Sprinkle on the herbs, olives, feta and hot pepper if using. At this point the salad may be made an hour ahead. If I cut the watermelon cubes early in the day, I keep in the fridge, but tomatoes don't hold up well in the fridge, so I add those when assembling the salad for serving.

In a small jar, add all the ingredients. Shake well and drizzle over the salad when ready to serve. Toss gently to mix so as not to break up the watermelon. Turn out onto a large serving platter or if bringing to a picnic, serve right out of a large container.

CHICKEN SALAD WITH SERRANO BASIL MAYO

When you are busy in the garden or life in general and it's too hot to cook, this is just the meal for one of those days. Even better, pack this up in a cooler and take it to the beach or a tailgate party!

Serves 2-3

▌INGREDIENTS

3 boneless chicken breasts, poached early in the day

3/4 cup toasted walnuts, chopped, save some for sprinkling on top, see **note** on toasting with the **basil pesto**

1/2 cup sweet onion, small diced

1/2 cup celery, small diced

1 serrano pepper, seeded and minced

2-3 tablespoons chives, minced, save some for sprinkling on top

1-2 radishes, sliced or cut into slivers for garnish

FOR POACHING THE CHICKEN:

▌INGREDIENTS

2 bay leaves

1 garlic clove, smashed

1/2 cup extra dry vermouth or any white wine, optional

Juice of 1/2 lemon

Pinch salt mix

Freshly ground black pepper

Place the chicken in a saucepan to fit in a single layer. Add all the ingredients and fill with water to cover chicken by 1-2 inches. Bring to a gentle simmer (you do not want a rolling boil here). Continue to simmer, turning the chicken over once about 20-25 minutes. You may also use bone in breasts of chicken but the cooking time will be longer. Remove to a plate and let cool. I like to strain and reserve the poaching liquid to use in soups or for cooking rice.

When chicken has cooled, cut into 1/2-1 inch pieces. Place in the fridge until ready to prepare the salad.

SERRANO BASIL MAYONNAISE

▌INGREDIENTS

About 2/3 cup mayonnaise, no measuring required

About 1 tablespoon Dijon mustard, no measuring required

1 serrano pepper, seeded and chopped

1 teaspoon sherry vinegar

1 large garlic clove

4-5 tops basil leaves

Pinch salt mix

Freshly ground black pepper

In a small food processor, add all the ingredients and blend well.

When ready to prepare the salad, add all other ingredients except the radishes to the prepared chicken, reserving some of the walnuts and chives for sprinkling on top. Add your desired amount of the serrano basil mayonnaise to moisten the chicken to your liking. Save extra for sandwiches.

Serve on a bed of red Russian kale leaves, roll up in any lettuce wrap of choice or serve on your favorite bread.

Note: This dressing also makes a great tea sandwich spread with chicken, salmon, or beef.

CAESAR MEATBALL WEDGE SALAD WITH DANDELION CROUTONS

We have been making many versions of this salad since the kids were little, and I must thank Rachel Ray for the idea! The kids always loved making the meatballs and this remains a family favorite to this day. I made this one night for myself and everyone wished they were home for it. Sorry Charlie!

Makes 9 meatballs or enough for 3 salads

FOR THE MEATBALLS:

▌INGREDIENTS

8-ounce prime rib burger, see **note**, or any ground beef

1 egg blended

1 tablespoon Dijon mustard

2 tablespoons parsley, chopped

2 tablespoons Parmigiano-Reggiano cheese, finely grated

1/8 cup **gluten-free Italian panko breadcrumbs**, see recipe, or any breadcrumbs

1 teaspoon olive oil

1 teaspoon dried oregano

1/2 teaspoon dried sweet basil or 1 tablespoon fresh basil, chopped

1/2 teaspoon gochugaru Korean chili flakes, see **my cupboard**, or any chili flakes

1/4 teaspoon garlic powder

Preheat oven to 400°F.

Prepare a baking sheet lined with parchment paper. In a medium bowl, add all the above ingredients and mix well. Using a one inch cookie scoop or tablespoon measure, form meatballs and place on the baking sheet. Bake until done about 20 minutes.

While meatballs are cooking, prepare the dressing and salad unless already made ahead.

Calvin, Nolan, Cristina 2007

continued $\longrightarrow$

CAESAR DRESSING

INGREDIENTS

1/3 cup mayonnaise

1/2 cup olive oil

1 tin anchovies, plus the oil
(minus 3 for topping the salad)

Heaping tablespoon Dijon mustard

Zest and juice of 1 lemon, at least
a 1/4 cup juice

3-4 small to medium garlic cloves

Splash Worcestershire sauce, optional

Few sprigs parsley

Freshly ground black pepper

In a small food processor, add garlic, parsley, mayonnaise and Dijon mustard. Blend well. Add in the anchovies, lemon juice, Worcestershire sauce and pepper. Blend again and with the machine running, slowly drizzle the olive oil through the top. Scrape down the sides of the bowl, taste for seasoning, perhaps adding a bit more lemon juice. We love it lemony! Blend a second more and pour into a glass container and store in the fridge until ready to top your salad.

When meatballs are done, remove from the oven and use a spoon to brush off adhered fat and set on a plate.

FOR THE SALAD:

INGREDIENTS

1/2 a romaine lettuce wedge, or up
to 3 halves depending on how
many you are serving

Chopped parsley for garnish

Chopped chives for garnish

Pecorino Romano cheese for
sprinkling on top

On a serving plate, add the romaine wedge and tuck in 3-4 meatballs. Roll the anchovies and place on the wedge. Drizzle over the dressing and place as many dandelion croutons as you like. Sprinkle on the chopped parsley and chives. Freshly grate a little Pecorino Romano cheese over the top with more freshly ground black pepper and serve.

Note: I order my prime rib burgers from Lobel's of New York. See **resources** for more information.

FOR THE DANDELION CROUTONS *see **Pan Fried Dandelion Flowers** on page 303*

TOMATOES AND GREENS SALAD WITH LEMON CREAM DRESSING

This is my kind of easy salad. Depending on how many people you want to serve, use a handful of greens per person and layer on the tomatoes!

Serves 4-6

INGREDIENTS

4 big handfuls mixed arugula and spinach, or your favorite lettuce mix

Any fresh ripe garden tomatoes of choice, sliced 1/2 inch thick

Handful cherry tomatoes

Chives and parsley, chopped for garnish

LEMON CREAM DRESSING

INGREDIENTS

1/4 cup extra virgin olive oil

Scant 1/4 cup mayonnaise

2 small garlic cloves, minced

2 1/2 tablespoons lemon juice, plus the zest of 1 lemon

Pinch salt mix

Freshly ground black pepper

In a jar, add all ingredients and any add ins of choice. Shake well and keep in the fridge until ready to top your salad. May be made ahead and kept in the fridge.

On a big platter, spread a bed of lettuce. Layer your tomato slices across the top. Top with the lemon cream dressing and serve.

ADD-INS OF CHOICE:

Small spoonful Dijon mustard, about a rounded teaspoon

1/2 tablespoon any herb of choice, finely minced, such as basil, chives, parsley or thyme

TUNA SALAD
IN AVOCADO BOATS

I absolutely live for tuna fish! Way back when a was a working girl outside the home, my favorite lunch was an open face tuna melt on a bagel. That's still amazing, but nowadays, we don't eat much tuna, so it is a real treat when we do have it. You know me – must have the potato chips!

Serves 1-2

▌INGREDIENTS

1 avocado peeled, sliced in half and pitted

1 4-ounce tin ventresca tuna in olive oil or 1-5 ounce can solid pack light tuna in olive oil

2 tablespoons or so mayonnaise, adding by the spoonful to moisten to your liking

1/4 cup red onion, finely diced, plus a little extra for garnish

1/4 cup Genovese basil, chopped, plus some small leaves for garnish

1/2 tablespoon lemon juice, plus a little more to rub over the avocados

2 small Thai chili peppers, seeded and minced or 1 hot cherry red pepper

1-2 tablespoons drained capers, chopped

1 tablespoon chives, chopped

1/2 yellow bell pepper or any color, diced for garnish

Freshly ground black pepper

Drain most of the oil from the tin and place tuna in a medium bowl. Add the mayonnaise and mix. Stir in the rest of the ingredients except the avocados. Taste for seasoning – most of the time it needs no salt, but if it needs a pinch, add it here. Take each avocado half and scoop out a little from the middle and rub some lemon juice all over to prevent from browning. Place on a serving plate and mound a scoop of the tuna in each avocado.

Dice up the avocado you scooped out and sprinkle on the tops and around the plate along with the bell pepper and extra onion. Add some freshly ground black pepper and serve.

soups & SANDWICHES

I was fortunate to grow up with some seriously amazing soup makers in my life and Mom always hit home with a warming bowl or a cool gazpacho. I love everything about making soups, the simmering and stirring of a nice hot soup or the beauty of a chilled soup - even serving in a shot glass for fun! Throw in a unique sandwich to eat on its own, or make it double the love and pair it with a flavorful soup.

CREAMY GREEN SPRING AND SUMMER GAZPACHO

Serve this in a small bowl alongside a meal or for a crowd, this makes the best cold shot to pass around to family and friends. An amuse-bouche in your backyard! One of my neighborhood buddies I grew up with and fellow recipe swapper, Frank Suher, begged the chef for this recipe from a place in Nantucket, Massachusetts. Original recipe made 2 quarts! We both revamped to downsize, plus, I made it gluten free and added in zucchini. Thanks, Frank!

▌ INGREDIENTS

3/4-1 pound cucumbers, peeled and seeded, cut into chunks

1 small zucchini, about 5-6 inches, peeled and seeded, cut into chunks

1 garlic clove, chopped

1/2 pound green grapes, washed

Heaping 2 tablespoons shallots, diced

1/4 of a bunch of cilantro with stalks, washed and trimmed, about a cup

3/4 of a large avocado, cut into chunks, use the last 1/4 to dice for garnish

2 tablespoons champagne vinegar

1/2 teaspoon salt mix

Lots of freshly ground black pepper

Serves 6 or more as a shot. In a high-speed blender, add ingredients in the order listed. Start blending on the lower speed and with your tamper, push the ingredients down. Then turn up the speed and blend until smooth. Store in a covered container in the refrigerator.

Serve cold straight out of the refrigerator, garnishing with extra diced avocado, cucumber or grapes. This recipe makes 3 cups, may be made a day ahead and is easily doubled.

GRILLED CHEESE AND TOMATO SANDWICHES WITH PARMIGIANO BREAD

I'm pretty sure you won't be whipping these up every day, but they sure make a nice treat to enjoy a fresh ripe juicy summer tomato. Crunchy, salty and sweet!

▌ INGREDIENTS

Each "sandwich" requires 2 tablespoons **Parmigiano-Reggiano cheese** *for each side, finely grated with a small hand grater or a box grater, as much as you need for as many sandwiches as you want to make.*

Fresh ripe garden tomatoes, sliced 1/4 inch thick

Basil leaves

Flake salt

Freshly ground black pepper

In a non-stick skillet, add 2 tablespoons cheese and pat into a circle. On low heat, melt and turn when it starts to get slightly brown. Flip with a thin spatula – if you can't get it to flip it's not ready yet. Flip and get the other side golden. Transfer to drain on paper towels.

Assemble the sandwiches by taking a cheese bread slice, layer a tomato slice, tiny pinch flake salt, as the cheese is salty, and freshly ground black pepper. Add a few basil leaves and top with another cheese bread slice. I guarantee you will eat these before sitting down.

ITALIAN ZUCCHINI MONTE CRISTO SANDWICHES

Our great friends Sara and Stan grow this amazing Italian zucchini with seeds they brought back from Italy years ago. I'm always lucky enough to get a few squash from them every summer. It is very meaty and great for cutting slices like bread.

INGREDIENTS

1 Italian zucchini, see *note*

Gruyère cheese slices or raw Monterey Jack style cheese

Basil leaves

1 egg blended with pinch of salt and pepper in a shallow bowl

Ham slices or prosciutto slices, optional

Butter and olive oil for pan frying

Note: You can use any large zucchini for this recipe. Cut lengthwise on a long zucchini and then cut those slices in half. Once you reach the seeds, cut slices from the other side.

Cut off the ends of the zucchini and peel. From the bottom end cut **1/8** inch slices crosswise until you reach the seeds. Keep two similar size pieces together. If making more than a few sandwiches, cut more slices from the other end. Save seeds for next years garden, if desired.

In a medium cast iron or non-stick pan set to medium, add a drizzle of olive oil and a small pat of butter. Dip 2 matching slices in the egg and then place in the pan when hot. Once browned on the one side, using two forks, flip the zucchini slice to the other side. On one zucchini slice, add 1 slice of cheese, a few basil leaves, 1 or 2 slices of ham and top with another slice of cheese. When the bottoms are browned, flip the empty slice over to the other slice making a sandwich. Transfer to a plate and rest a bit before slicing. These sandwiches are a nice pair served with my roasted garden tomato soup.

ROASTED TOMATO SOUP

*When you have an abundance of tomatoes or tomatoes the birds have pecked at, this soup helps put them to good use, and a small bowl goes perfectly with the **Italian zucchini Monte Cristo sandwiches.***

▌ INGREDIENTS

3 pounds garden or farmers market variety heirloom tomatoes such as, Grampy's Italian heirloom, Nebraska wedding, black zebra, costoluto Genovese, purple Cherokee, or any combo, seeded

2 full tops Genovese basil, about 12-14 leaves

6 garlic cloves, sliced in half

1 sprig rosemary

2-3 tablespoons extra virgin olive oil

1/2 teaspoon salt

1/4 teaspoon sugar

Freshly ground black pepper

1 cup finely grated Parmigiano-Reggiano cheese, loosely packed

Preheat oven to 350°F. Cut tomatoes into chunks and add to a medium sized non-reactive bowl. Add in the basil leaves, garlic cloves, and sprig of rosemary. Sprinkle with the salt, sugar and pepper. Drizzle with the oil and sprinkle on the salt and sugar. Toss with your hands to coat well. Turn out onto a baking sheet and roast for 20 minutes. Remove from the oven and with a large spatula mix around the tomatoes trying to keep the basil tucked under the tomatoes. Place back in the oven and roast another 20 minutes.

Let cool and then scrape all into a high-speed blender, including the juices. Blend well and return soup to an enameled saucepan. May be made ahead at this point. Refrigerate and when ready to serve, warm gently and add in the cheese, stirring until melted. Taste for seasoning, adding a bit more pepper if necessary. Serve with an extra grating of cheese and a few little basil leaves.

OPEN FACE SALMON SALAD MELTS ON PERSIMMON TOMATO BREAD

The warm tomatoes get so juicy and with the melty cheese - such a surprising combo and you won't even miss the bread!

▌ **INGREDIENTS**

2 6-ounce cans wild Alaskan pink Salmon, boneless and skinless, drained

Mayonnaise to moisten to your liking

1 hot cherry red pepper, seeded and chopped, saving some for garnish

1/2 cup white onion, finely diced, or any onion

1/2 cup parsley, chopped

Pinch flake salt

Freshly ground black pepper

3 large persimmon heirloom tomatoes, or any large variety like carbon, beefsteak or Grampy Italian heirloom, sliced into 1/4-1/2 inch thick slices, removing seeds if preferred

Couple handfuls arugula or any lettuce you like

Dubliner cheese, cut into thin slices, or any of your favorite cheese

Serve 3 tomato slices per person – salmon salad serves enough for 4. **Preheat oven or toaster oven to 400°F.** In a medium bowl, add the salmon with enough mayonnaise to moisten to your liking. Stir in the cherry pepper, onion, parsley, salt, pepper, and mix well.

Line a baking tray with parchment paper. Place the tomato slices on the parchment and top each with some arugula leaves. Then top with a spoonful of the salmon salad spreading evenly. Add a few slices of the cheese and bake for 10 minutes, then turn to broil for 3-5 minutes until golden, being sure to keep an eye. Remove from the oven and let sit a few minutes before removing with a spatula to individual plates. Sprinkle with extra chopped parsley and hot cherry red peppers. Eat with a knife and fork and a side of your favorite crunch factor.

BLG SANDWICH
BACON, LETTUCE AND GUACAMOLE

When the cat's away, the mouse needs something a little lighter to eat...my husband, Roby, loves his baseball, hockey and football games, and when he's out at any given one, you can bet one of my "go to" meals is this BLG with **thick cut potato chips.**

▌ INGREDIENTS

4 romaine lettuce leaves per sandwich

2-3 pieces **baked bacon**

1 recipe **guacamole**, or your favorite guacamole, see **note next page**

Mayonnaise, optional

Chopped dill or any herb of choice

Thick cut potato chips, see recipe.

Take two leaves for the bottom, resting one on the other with the tops facing the outside. Do this for the top too. Spread the guacamole on the bottom leaves, add a couple pieces of bacon, then sprinkle on some dill or any herb of choice. Spread some mayonnaise on the upper leaves, if desired, and place the top on to make your sandwich. Cut in half and enjoy with the thick cut potato chips if desired.

For a vegetarian version, add cucumber slices for the bacon. Later in the season add the T for tomato.

GUACAMOLE

Serves 4

▍INGREDIENTS

1/2 tablespoon fresh lemon juice

1 1/2 tablespoons fresh lime juice

1/2 teaspoon coarse grey sea salt

2 Hass avocados, ripened, halved and skinned, seed removed

2 scallions, finely diced

1 garlic clove, minced

1-2 jalapeño or serrano peppers, seeds removed, minced

1/2 cup cilantro, chopped

1/2 teaspoon ground cumin

1/4 teaspoon dried epazote, or about a 1/2 tablespoon fresh, chopped, optional

In a medium bowl, add the lemon juice, lime juice, and salt. Add in the avocado halves and break up with the side of your fork and mix through the lemon and lime juice. I don't completely mash at this point because with each addition, the guacamole gets mashed more and if you like it chunky, it will get over mixed. Stir in the scallions, garlic, hot pepper of choice, cilantro, cumin and epazote. At this point mash to your desired consistency. Taste for seasoning adding more lime juice or salt if necessary. Cover and refrigerate until serving.

Note: We all make guacamole in our house and everyone makes it their own special way. My son Calvin likes adding red onions and uses a potato masher. None of us are shy on heat and we use a variety of hot peppers. Especially in winter, we reach for the frozen, seeded variety in the ice cube trays. See **miscellaneous** for tips on freezing peppers.

VEGETARIAN CAULIFLOWER SOUP

I made this for my good friend Jan when she was under the weather and she insisted I put the recipe in the book. It's a warm and comforting soup anytime.

Serves 6

🔖 INGREDIENTS

1 large head cauliflower, cut into florets (save stalks for another use)

2 cups sweet onion, diced about 1 large, such as vidalia

3 extra large garlic cloves, large mince

1 tablespoon butter

1 tablespoon olive oil

1/2 teaspoon Herbes de Provence

1 bay leaf

2 small Yukon gold potatoes, peeled and cut into small cubes, about 1/2 inch

32 ounces organic vegetable broth

Pecorino Romano cheese, grated

Drizzle of your best extra virgin olive oil

1 teaspoon fresh chopped rosemary

Freshly ground black pepper

In a large soup pot, sauté the onions in the butter and olive oil for about 5-7 minutes. Season with a little salt and pepper. Add in the garlic, Herbes de Provence and bay leaf, and sauté a few minutes more. Add in the cauliflower florets and the cubed potato. Pour in the vegetable broth and simmer, stirring every now and again, about 45 minutes.

Test the cauliflower and potato to see if they are very soft. Remove from the heat and with an immersion blender, blend until nice and creamy. Taste for seasoning and ladle into bowls with a sprinkling of the fresh rosemary, a sprinkling of the Pecorino Romano cheese, and a drizzle of your best olive oil. Serve with a nice slice of your favorite bread.

LEEK AND LOVAGE SOUP

Every spring, the lovage is one of the first herbs to pop up along with the chives. Its flavor is sort of like a cross between strong celery and dill. When you brush up against the plant, the fragrance is extraordinary! Use the tender spring leaves for this soup. You will love the creaminess from the potatoes. And even more cool, the stalks are hollow and they make a neat way to serve the soup with a lovage straw. Cut the straws from the thick ends of the stalks.

INGREDIENTS

2 1/2 cups leeks, diced, about 1 1/2 to 2 large, white and pale green parts

2 garlic cloves, chopped

1 tablespoon butter

1 tablespoon olive oil

1 cup lovage leaves, lightly packed, reserving stalks to make straws, if desired

2 medium Yukon gold potatoes, peeled and cubed

4 cups chicken stock, or keep vegetarian by using veggie broth

In a medium stock pot, add butter and oil. Bring heat to just under medium and add leeks, a pinch of salt, and freshly ground black pepper. Sauté about 5-7 minutes being sure not to brown them. Add the garlic, potatoes, lovage leaves and another tiny pinch of salt and black pepper.

Continue to stir and sauté until lovage leaves turn a bright green, about 5 minutes more. At this point, add the chicken broth, simmering and stirring every so often, about 15 minutes more, or until potatoes are very tender. Using an immersion blender (or a blender), blend until nice and creamy. I find it doesn't need more salt as the chicken broth is salty. Serve in pretty bowls with the lovage straw.

OPEN FACE BLTP SANDWICH
BACON, LETTUCE, TOMATO, AND PEACH

*When we have a nice ripe tomato or two, there's nothing better than a good old fashioned BLT. I happened to have some ripe peaches and thought hmmm, should I? Yes, I should and glad I did! Make the **baked bacon** and everyone can assemble their own sandwich.*

▌ INGREDIENTS

1 toasted slice of your favorite
   bread, or 2 if you want a
   topper

Mayonnaise

Few leaves of lettuce

Basil leaves

Mint leaves

Few thin slices peach, peeled

Few thin slices tomato

2 slices cooked Niman Ranch
   maple bacon

Freshly ground black pepper

To build your sandwich, take the toasted bread and spread on the mayonnaise. Layer on the lettuce, basil and mint leaves. Evenly distribute the peach slices and then the tomato slices. Add a sprinkle of freshly ground black pepper and then top with the bacon. The mint and the peach, together with the juicy tomato and salty bacon is divine. Feel free to add a top.

ROASTED TOMATOES BRUSCHETTA

Bruschetta just means Italian toasted bread and I make it so many different ways. I make one loaf for company and one for family on gluten-free French bread. It will always be a winner. The aroma of the tomatoes while roasting is incredible!

FOR THE TOMATOES

▍INGREDIENTS

3-4 Cherokee purple tomatoes and carbon tomatoes, seeded and cubed, or any tomatoes

2 tops Genovese basil, about 12-14 leaves

3 garlic cloves, each cut in half

1/2 teaspoon Mexican oregano

Pinch flake salt or grey sea salt

Freshly ground black pepper

Drizzle of olive oil

Preheat oven to 350°F or toaster oven to 365°F. Lightly spray your baking sheet (do not line with foil when roasting tomatoes). In a medium to large bowl, add the tomatoes, and the rest of the ingredients.

Toss gently to mix and spread out in a single layer on the baking sheet. Try to tuck the basil leaves under the tomatoes. Roast for 30 minutes. When tomatoes have cooled a bit, add to a food processor and pulse blend leaving the tomatoes chunky.

FOR THE BRUSCHETTA

No one can resist a crispy piece of this bruschetta. Pump it up even more with a layer of any pesto before topping with the tomatoes, and then sprinkle on the cheese.

▍INGREDIENTS

1 loaf ciabatta bread

Your best extra virgin olive oil

1 to 2 garlic clove cloves, whole

Any pesto if desired

Roasted tomatoes

Pecorino Romano cheese

Slice the ciabatta bread in half horizontally. Rub with olive oil and grill on low heat, oil side down for 5-7 minutes until just golden, or broil in the oven until just golden. Remove to a cutting board and while warm, take a garlic clove and rub it over the surface of both slices of the bread. Spread a layer of pesto if desired or just top with tomatoes.

Sprinkle with a little Pecorino Romano cheese and place back in the oven for a few minutes to warm the pesto and cheese. Remove and slice into 4-5 slices per side. Makes an excellent addition to any meal or cut into smaller pieces and serve as a hors d'oeuvre.

dinnertime

It's funny – what goes around comes around. My kids now text me from college or their home to ask me how to make a specific recipe, or to request a long-time favorite dinner dish for me to make when they are headed home, and I love it! 99 birthday dinners later – what would you request? Here are some of our best-loved dishes made time and time again!

CHICKEN PARMIGIANA

This is one of the many requested recipes by my super kids and I'm always happy to make it because my husband and I love it too. It takes a bit of prep, but if you have the homemade breadcrumbs in the freezer and a jar of sauce in your cupboard, you will be good to go.

Serves 3 and easily doubled for 6

INGREDIENTS

Grapeseed oil as needed for pan frying

1 24-ounce jar Rao's Arrabbiata sauce or Marinara sauce warming on the stove

1 container of fresh mozzarella, small golf-size balls, cut into thirds

Small hunk Parmigiano-Reggiano cheese for grating

2 eggs blended in one pie plate

1 cup **gluten-free Italian seasoned breadcrumbs** added to another pie plate, add more as needed (that way all of the crumbs don't get contaminated with the raw chicken and you are able to use any leftover crumbs), or any breadcrumbs

1 3-pack skinless, boneless chicken breasts, cut out tendon, trim fat, butterfly like a book and pound thin, almost plate size, see **note** on next page

Chopped dill, parsley or basil for garnish

Preheat oven to 400°F. When ready to get cooking, have a baking sheet lightly sprayed with oil and large enough to hold all the chicken next to your stove, as well as a couple stacked paper towels.

In two non-stick skillets, (I prefer over cast iron for this as it gets too hot and can easily burn.) heat up a shear layer of grapeseed oil on medium to a notch or two over medium heat, but not too hot.

Dredge a piece of chicken in the egg and then into the crumbs, patting to coat well. Feel free to double dip if you have enough crumbs. Pan fry until golden turning only once, then flip and get the other side golden. When done, using a large spatula, set the chicken on the paper towels to blot the grease and then place on the baking sheet. When all the chicken are on the baking sheet, spoon on your tomato sauce of choice and spread over each cutlet. Hand grate a layer of Parmigiano and then distribute evenly the fresh cut mozzarella.

Place in the oven for 10 minutes. Then turn to broil and WATCH until cheese gets golden bubbles about 2 minutes – seriously don't turn your back. Remove from the oven and transfer to individual plates. Sprinkle with fresh dill, parsley, or basil.

Note: To remove the tendon, take hold of it from the end with one hand and with the other hand, scrape your knife along the tendon until it comes right out. To butterfly chicken, lay the thickest part of the breast vertical at the top. Place your hand flat on the top and with your knife, cut horizontally into the thickest part but don't go all the way through.

Place the butterflied breast between a long sheet of plastic wrap or in a large zip top bag set on a cutting board and pound thin, being careful not tear the chicken. Set each one on a plate. This is a step that I like doing earlier in the day, so when I'm ready to get cooking, it's all ready to go. Cover and keep in the fridge. If you double the recipe, you may need to use two baking sheets.

BAKED "FRIED" CHICKEN

We love fried chicken and make it especially for Derby Day for our dear special friend Norma, who is considered family. She always used to make it for us in her cast iron pans which years ago, she has since given to me. So, the tables have turned, and we have taken over making it, but wanted a lighter and less messy way to make it. Everyone seems to enjoy it and the skin gets nice and crispy.

Serves 6

FOR THE CHICKEN

▌ INGREDIENTS

1 family pack chicken thighs, bone in and skin on, trimmed of excess fat, about 11-12 pieces

2 cups **homemade buttermilk,** or any buttermilk

3 tablespoons **habanero Heaven hot sauce,** or any of your favorite hot sauce

1 teaspoon salt mix

Freshly ground black pepper

4-6 large leaves basil, chopped for garnish

Place chicken in a large non-reactive bowl. In a medium bowl, add 2 cups buttermilk, the hot sauce, salt and pepper and mix well. Pour over the chicken and with a spatula toss to coat well.

If the chicken is not covered by the buttermilk, add more to cover plus more hot sauce if you want. Cover and marinate at least 6 hours or overnight but absolutely can do off the cuff in 1-2 hours.

Bring to room temperature before cooking, about 20 minutes.

FOR THE DRY INGREDIENTS

▌ INGREDIENTS

2 cups gluten-free flour, Bob's red mill 1 to 1 baking flour, or any flour

1 cup **gluten-free Italian seasoned breadcrumbs,** or your favorite breadcrumbs

1/2 tablespoon smoked paprika, hot or sweet

1/2 tablespoon chili powder

1/2 tablespoon dried oregano

1 teaspoon salt mix

1 teaspoon garlic powder

Freshly ground black pepper

Mix all of the ingredients in a medium bowl and pour into a double bagged brown lunch bag. **Preheat oven to 425°F.** Prepare a broiler pan, lining the bottom pan with foil to save on cleanup and lightly spray the top pan with cooking spray. With tongs, add 2 thighs at a time, draining as much butter-milk as you can, then add to the bag with the dry ingredients. Fold down the bag and shake, coating the chicken well. Using another pair of tongs, take the chicken out one at a time and lay skin side up on the broiler pan leaving space between each one. Do the same until all are done. Lightly spray tops and sides with cooking spray and place in the oven on the middle rack.

Set timer for 30 minutes. Check and rotate pan, baking another 30 minutes, which is generally perfect tim-ing in my oven, but every oven varies, so keep an eye. Transfer to a serving platter and sprinkle with sliced basil. This got a yum review!

STUFFED CHICKEN BREASTS WITH SPINACH

My son Calvin loved to request this chicken when he was headed home from college or for a birthday dinner. When he was little, it didn't matter if he was eating steak or salmon, he always said, "I really love this chicken, Mom!"

Serves 4

INGREDIENTS

4-6 chicken breasts, tendon removed, butterfly like a book and pound thin, see **note** with **chicken parmigiana**

1/2 cup cream cheese, room temperature

1/2 cup sour cream

10 ounces frozen spinach, squeezed of liquid and chopped

4 scallions, diced fine

2 large garlic cloves, minced

Zest of 1 lemon, about 1 1/2 teaspoons

2 tablespoons lemon juice

Grating of nutmeg, about 1/8 teaspoon

1 tablespoon chives, chopped, plus more for garnish

1 teaspoon grey salt

Freshly ground black pepper

2 tablespoons butter

1/2-3/4 cups **gluten-free breadcrumbs,** or any breadcrumbs, optional

Lemon wedges for serving

Add all ingredients except chicken, butter, lemon wedges and breadcrumbs to a medium bowl and mix well. Makes enough filling for six breasts at **1/4** cup filling per breast. I like to spread out a large piece of foil on the counter and lay the chicken pieces horizontally. Portion the stuffing and place on the right side of breast leaving a **1/4** inch edge, then fold over the other side and lightly press down over the filling. Don't worry if you overstuff and some comes out during cooking. As each are done, carefully place on a baking sheet.

Preheat oven to 425°F.

Melt the butter and brush the tops of the chicken all over and sprinkle on some breadcrumbs, if desired and then, drizzle with a little more butter. Season with a little pinch of salt and freshly ground black pepper. Place in the oven and cook 20 minutes. Rotate pan and cook 10 minutes more and they should be nicely cooked and golden. Remove to serving platter and let chicken rest about 5 minutes. Sprinkle with chives and serve with lemon wedges.

BUFFALO CHICKEN TENDERS

*I came up with this gluten-free version years ago when the kids weren't able to order them in a restaurant. They were much younger then, and what kid doesn't love chicken tenders? Even though the kids are all grown up, we still love them. Try them on the **iceberg wedge salad with feta dressing** or they are simply great on their own. My guys get psyched if I make them for Super Bowl Sunday! Even if you don't make the salad, the feta dressing is a great dipper. Be forewarned, the recipe takes a bit of timing and they don't last long! Recipe is easily doubled or tripled.*

Serves 4 as an appetizer with other treats or 2 per person

FOR THE CHICKEN

▌ INGREDIENTS

- 8 chicken tenders with tendons removed, see **note** with **chicken parmigiana**, or slice 3 breasts lengthwise into thirds

- 1/4 cup of **habanero heaven hot sauce,** or your favorite hot sauce

- 1 cup **homemade buttermilk**, or any buttermilk

In a small glass bowl, add the hot sauce and the buttermilk and mix well. In shallow glass dish in one layer add the tenders and cover with the buttermilk mixture making sure they all are covered. Marinate in the refrigerator at least 4 hours or overnight.

FOR THE COATING

In another glass bowl add the following ingredients and set aside until ready to dip.

▌ INGREDIENTS

- 1 cup gluten-free flour, Bob's red mill 1 to 1 baking flour, or any flour

- 1 teaspoon hot smoked paprika

- 2 teaspoons garlic powder

- 1 teaspoon onion powder

- 1 teaspoon salt mix

- 1/2 teaspoon black pepper

Prepare a baking sheet with parchment or foil and set a wire rack on top. Take each tender and let the buttermilk drip off the chicken and dip in the flour mixture. Dip back into the buttermilk mixture, then back into the flour, shaking off excess. (My kids like them double dipped, but you could dip once if preferred.) Lay each one on the rack and when all are finished, let the chicken rest at room temperature for 15 minutes or so to let them dry out a bit and let coating adhere. If you cook them right away they are too pasty.

FOR PAN FRYING THE CHICKEN

▌INGREDIENTS

**Grapeseed oil or Refined
   Coconut Oil**

Start dipping one hour before pan frying. I like to start dipping at about 5pm – it takes about 15-20 minutes to dip 8 pieces. At 6pm I begin to pan fry in batches. (Or adjust timing to whenever you want to cook them.) In a large non-stick skillet on medium heat, add a thin layer of oil. When pan is hot, add the chicken and pan fry about 4 minutes per side.

Take care to make sure the pan doesn't get too hot, so the chicken doesn't burn, but also not too low that the chicken absorbs a lot of oil. Be sure to turn chicken to brown on wider edges. Drain on paper towels, sprinkle with salt and chives. Serve with the salad, if desired, or on their own with your favorite dipping sauce.

PARMIGIANO CRUSTED TURKEY CAL PAILLARDS

As always, I love a great one platter meal. This dish is named for my son Calvin who requested something like this for dinner one summer evening.

Serves 5 or 3 with leftovers

▌ INGREDIENTS

2 packs, or 2 pounds turkey tenderloins, pounded thin

Drizzle of olive oil

6-8 ounce hunk Parmigiano-Reggiano cheese, finely grated

1 teaspoon salt mix

1/2 heaping cup gluten-free flour, Bob's red mill 1 to 1 baking flour, or any flour

3 large egg whites, reserve 2 yolks for making the *arugula salad with creamy dressing,* if desired

4-5 handfuls arugula

Preheat oven to 450°F. Set a baking sheet rubbed with olive oil near your work space to place each tenderloin on after dipping. In a pie plate, mix Parmigiano cheese, salt, and gluten-free flour. In a separate dish, whisk the egg whites until foamy. Dip each tenderloin in the egg whites and then press into the cheese mixture, coating well. Lay each one on the prepared baking sheet.

Place baking sheet in the oven on the middle rack and cook for 10 minutes. Flip and cook 5 minutes more. If not golden, broil for 2 minutes keeping an eye on them. For serving, on a large platter, arrange a bed of baby arugula and drizzle with the creamy dressing. Top with the turkey in a row down the center. Place lemon wedges around and top with basil pesto, if desired, and serve with extra creamy dressing on the side.

FOR THE CREAMY DRESSING

*If you're not a fan of using raw eggs, see **note** or the alternative recipe without raw eggs, **lemon cream dressing.***

▌ INGREDIENTS

2 large egg yolks (whites used above in the paillards)

1 large garlic clove

Juice of 2 lemons

1/2 cup extra virgin olive oil

1/4 teaspoon salt mix if necessary, taste first before adding

Freshly ground black pepper

In a small food processor, blend yolks, garlic and lemon juice. Add the olive oil **1/4** cup at a time through the top, blending well after each addition. Taste and add the salt if needed. Keep in the fridge until serving.

Note: When using raw eggs, I am just sure to have fresh bought organic pasture raised eggs which I rinse and dry thoroughly before cracking.

TURKEY SCALLOPINI FRANCESE

Growing up, my Nana made a helluva mind-blowing Francese and it was my most favorite thing to order in an Italian restaurant. We traditionally make this with veal, but it is equally delicious with turkey or chicken.

Serves 6

▌ INGREDIENTS

2 packs, or 2 pounds turkey tenderloins, pounded thin

Grapeseed oil as needed for cooking

4 eggs

1 cup gluten-free flour, Bob's red mill all-purpose baking flour, or any flour

1 teaspoon salt mix

Freshly ground black pepper

Chopped chives and chive flowers for garnish

Lemon wedges for garnish

FOR THE PAN SAUCE

2/3 cup extra dry vermouth

1 lemon juiced

1/2 cup chicken broth

1 tablespoon tapioca starch

1 tablespoon water

Spread a long piece of plastic wrap on a cutting board and place 2 tenderloins at a time on top. Fold over the wrap and pound each tenderloin until thin and place on a platter. Repeat with the remaining tenderloins. I like to do this ahead of time so that when I am ready to get cooking, this part is done. Keep in the refrigerator until ready to cook.

Preheat oven to 300°F. When ready to get cooking, in a pie plate, add the 4 eggs and beat to blend. In another pie plate or shallow dish, add the flour, salt and pepper. Have a folded paper towel and baking sheet ready to go next to the stove for quickly blotting any excess grease, and then to place the tenderloins on when they have finished cooking to keep warm in the oven.

In a large nonstick skillet, drizzle in some grapeseed oil. When the pan is medium, but not high heat, dredge the tenderloins in the flour, shaking off the excess and then dip in the egg, coating both sides and letting the excess drip off, then place in the skillet. Cook shaking the pan and drizzling a little more oil if necessary. Cook the tenderloins until golden on one side, and then flip to the other side, turning only once. Repeat with the remaining tenderloins, wiping out the pan if necessary before adding more oil. Place tenderloins on the baking sheet and keep warm in the preheated oven until all are cooked.

Wipe the skillet of any blackened crumbs and oil and return to the heat. Add the vermouth, lemon juice and chicken broth. Cook, whisking on just over medium heat to reduce a little. Then, in a small bowl, mix the tapioca starch and the water and with a whisk add to the simmering broth. Continue to stir until thickened, about 1-2 minutes. Taste for seasoning and remove from the heat.

Remove tenderloins from the oven and place on a serving platter. Pour the sauce over the tenderloins and garnish with fresh chopped chives, flowers and lemon wedges.

TURKEY BURGERS FOR THE 4TH

These burgers are awesome on the grill! They feed a crowd, but if you don't want too many, just cut the recipe in half. But I wouldn't wait for July 4th to make these, they are perfect anytime!

Makes 13 burgers (serves 9 plus leftovers)

▐ INGREDIENTS

4 packs, or 4 pounds 75% lean ground turkey

1/2 bunch cilantro, plus stalks, minced

1/4 bunch parsley, plus stalks, minced

4 large garlic cloves, minced

2 red apples (Granny Smith green apples are also great), peeled and diced very fine

2 large spoonfuls Dijon mustard, about 4 tablespoons

Juice of 1 lime, about 2 tablespoons

2-3 tablespoons extra virgin olive oil

1 teaspoon salt mix

Freshly ground black pepper

Coconut oil spray

Prepare a baking sheet lined with parchment or waxed paper. In a large bowl, mix all the ingredients except the ground turkey and oil spray. Then add the ground turkey and mix well. Using a **1/2** cup measure to portion (see **note** on next page), scoop the turkey and turn out into your hands to form into patties and place each patty in one layer onto the baking sheet. When first layer is full, top with another piece of parchment and continue until all patties are made. Burgers can be made ahead at this point and kept in the fridge, but also refrigerate at least 30-60 minutes before grilling.

Spray the burger tops with the coconut oil spray and place that side first on a medium heat grill. These will not take long to cook, about 4 minutes per side, but each grill is different, so timing may differ. When you flip the burgers, add the cheese, if desired. When all are done, remove to a platter and serve with the toppings and lemon chive mayonnaise, or any of your favorite toppings.

The kids when they were little on the 4th of July.

LEMON CHIVE MAYONNAISE

▌INGREDIENTS

1 cup mayonnaise or thereabouts, no need to measure

1 1/2 tablespoons lemon juice

1 1/2 tablespoons fresh chives, minced

1/8 teaspoon rosemary, minced

Tiny pinch salt mix

Freshly ground black pepper

FOR SERVING THE BURGERS

Dubliner Cheddar cheese, or any of your favorite cheese

Any lettuce of choice

Tomato slices

Lemon chive mayonnaise

Your favorite burger buns, or try the *zucchini cake fritters* as buns

Mix well in a small bowl adding more lemon juice if desired. Serve alongside the burgers.

Note: When making and type of burger or fish cake, I love using measuring cups to portion so that they are all the same size. Give the measuring cup a quick oil spray so mixture comes out easily and wet your hands with a splash of water to form the burgers so the meat doesn't stick.

PECAN CRUSTED
BUFFALO TURKEY TENDERLOINS

These make such an easy weeknight meal with a great salad. I pop them right in my toaster oven.

Serves 2 with leftovers for the lunchbox

🚩 INGREDIENTS

1 pack, or 1 pound turkey tenderloins

About 1/4 cup mayonnaise, no measuring required

About 1/4 cup Dijon mustard, no measuring required

1 1/2 tablespoons *habanero Heaven hot sauce,* or any hot sauce

1/2 teaspoon dried thyme

Pinch salt mix

Freshly ground black pepper

Mix together all ingredients except the turkey and add to a pie plate or shallow dish.

FOR THE
PECAN COATING

🚩 INGREDIENTS

2 cups raw pecans, fresh or out of the freezer

1 teaspoon dried thyme or 2 tablespoons fresh if you have it

1 large garlic clove

Pinch salt

Freshly ground black pepper

In a small food processor, pulse blend ingredients for pecan mixture until coarsely chopped. Set out into a another pie plate or shallow dish to dip tenderloins.

Preheat oven to 425°F. Dip each tenderloin generously in the sauce mixture and press into the pecan mixture. Lay each on a lightly sprayed baking sheet.

Place in the oven and bake 20-22 minutes. Transfer to serving platter and garnish with lemon wedges.

PORTERHOUSE STEAKS ON THE GRILL

It's nice having kids that can drive because while I was home making the chimichurri sauce, my son Nolan was happy to go pick up and then grill the steaks.

◣ INGREDIENTS

Two 1 1/2-inch thick grass-fed porterhouse steaks

Peruvian salt, or your favorite salt, patted in on both sides

Tons of freshly ground black pepper

Preheat gas grill to medium heat.

Place the steaks on the grill and cook for 6 minutes, then using tongs, turn to rotate halfway to get crosshatch, another 6 minutes. Flip and grill 3 minutes, then turn to rotate halfway to get crosshatch, another 3 minutes. Place on a platter and rest for 10-15 minutes. Serve with the **basil cilantro chimichurri,** or any you choose would be a winner!

BOURSIN BURGERS

Can you tell we love our boursin spread? My son Nolan is "burger boy", and we both love making them for friends and family. This is a nice surprise when someone least expects it, but feel free to make the burgers without the stuffing. They are fabulous either way. The burgers, made without the stuffing, was a go to when the kids had friends over to dinner. When served that way, we love setting up a burger bar with tons of fixins. Makes 12 burgers.

INGREDIENTS

1 recipe *boursin cheese spread*

3 pounds grass-fed ground beef

2 eggs, blended

1 heaping spoonful, about 2 tablespoons Dijon mustard

1 tablespoon extra-virgin olive oil

1/4 teaspoon my dried ground Asian peppers, or any dried ground chili peppers, optional

1 teaspoon lava salt or salt mix

Lots of fresh ground black pepper

1/2 tablespoon ground coriander

1/2 teaspoon onion powder

1/2 teaspoon garlic powder

Any sliced fresh ripe tomatoes and greens

Sliced onion for tops of burgers, optional

Fresh dill for garnish

In a large bowl, add all the ingredients except the beef, boursin cheese spread and the garnishes and blend well. Then, add the beef and mix well, but not so much as to overwork the meat.

Preheat grill to 350°F. Prepare a baking sheet lined with foil and then topped with parchment. If stuffing, use a **1/4** cup measure to portion, scoop and form burgers with your hands making piles of two for each burger and place on a baking sheet. On the bottom burger press an indent in the middle and add a **1/2** tablespoon of the boursin cheese spread. Place the other half of the burger on top, and with your hands, pat and seal the burgers together so the cheese stays inside. I find 4 people end up eating 6 burgers! No kidding! If choosing not to stuff, form by using **1/2** cup measure.

Grill 8 minutes one side, then flip and grill 8-10 minutes on the other side. Let rest and serve with special sauce and your favorite buns.

FOR THE SPECIAL SAUCE

INGREDIENTS

1/2 cup ketchup

1/4 cup mayonnaise

3 tablespoons horseradish

1/2 tablespoon lemon juice

1/2 tablespoon Dijon mustard

Splash of any hot sauce, optional

Mix all ingredients in a small bowl and keep in the fridge until serving.

DRY AGED BONE-IN RIBEYES

Quite possibly some of the best steaks I've had thanks to my son Calvin picking these out by accident from the dry aged steak counter.

Serves 4 with leftovers – these are thick steaks!

FOR THE STEAKS

INGREDIENTS

2 3-inch dry aged ribeye steaks

Arbequina olive oil, or any
   olive oil

3-4 long sprigs rosemary, about
   1/4 cup, minced

Truffle salt and grey coarse sea
   salt

Freshly ground black pepper

Place the steaks on a foil lined baking sheet. Rub about a teaspoon of oil on each side. I pour the oil onto a spoon and then drizzle on the steak using the back of the spoon to spread the oil around. Then, sprinkle the rosemary, salt and pepper evenly on each side, pressing into the meat.

Heat and scrape down the grill. On medium heat, add the steaks. Set a timer for 6 minutes. With tongs, rotate to get the crosshatch another 6 minutes. Flip the steaks and set timer for 6 minutes, then rotate another 6 minutes to get the crosshatch. Take off the grill and rest on a platter 10-12 minutes. These were perfect medium, but if you like your steaks on the rarer side, cut the time to 4-5 minutes. Serve with the horseradish sauce, if desired.

FOR THE HORSERADISH SAUCE

INGREDIENTS

About 1/2 cup sour cream

2 tablespoons horseradish, not
   cream style

1 tablespoon lemon juice

Pinch salt mix

Freshly ground black pepper

Mix all ingredients in a small bowl and serve alongside the beef. Also makes a nice sandwich spread with any leftover steak.

SURF AND TURF

This makes a fantastic special meal for any occasion, but this particular night happened to be our anniversary dinner. Lucky our son Nolan was home, or should I say he was lucky to be home? This would also make a great Valentine's dinner.

Serves 4

FOR THE SURF

⚑ INGREDIENTS

3 fresh Maine lobster tails, or frozen, defrosted overnight in the fridge, see **note**

Truffle butter or Tuscan herb butter

1/2 cup extra dry vermouth or any white wine

Preheat oven to 425°F. Stuff some butter in the tail and place all on a baking sheet. Add the vermouth to the pan. Bake on the rack closer to the top of the oven for 15 minutes. Put these in the oven a few minutes before you put the steaks on the grill and while the meat rests, the lobster tails will finish cooking. When tails are done, remove to a platter so they don't continue to cook.

FOR THE TURF

⚑ INGREDIENTS

3 boneless ribeye steaks

Carolina hickory salt

Smoked sea salt

Freshly ground black pepper

Fresh dill for garnish

Season steaks with your favorite salt; here I love Carolina hickory and smoked sea salt for that smoky flavor and grind on plenty of black pepper. Grill on medium heat 5 minutes per side, but this will depend on the thickness of your steak, and how you like it cooked. When done, remove steaks to a platter and let them rest about 10 minutes.

FOR THE POTATOES

⚑ INGREDIENTS

5 medium Yukon gold potatoes, washed and pierced with a knife

Bake 1 hour at **425°F** in the toaster oven or middle rack of the oven below the lobster tails. I just like using the toaster oven as it has its own timer.

FOR THE EASY MIXED SALAD

▌INGREDIENTS

Handful of your favorite greens per person

Your best extra virgin olive oil and a small dash of truffle oil, optional

Juice of half a lemon, about a tablespoon or two

Pinch of Italian seasoning

Pinch of dried oregano

Pinch of flake salt

Freshly ground black pepper

In a medium sized serving bowl, add in the greens. Then, drizzle with extra virgin olive oil and just a dash of truffle oil, if desired. Squeeze over some lemon juice, then sprinkle on a pinch of Italian seasoning and dried oregano. Top with a pinch of flake salt and freshly ground black pepper. Toss and serve with the meal.

For assembly, on each dinner plate, arrange a steak and lobster tail. Place a baked potato and dress with the truffle butter, or Tuscan herb butter, and black pepper. Add sour cream if desired. Add a portion of the salad and serve.

Note: If you're lucky enough to get some fresh Maine lobster tails then you are rockin! But, if not, I order from Lobel's of New York, as well as the specialty butters, see **resources**.

NOLAN'S FLAMING AU POIVRE TENDERLOINS

All 3 of my kids have been cooking since they were old enough to sit up. Nolan, my boy scout and tech guy, loves equipment and made these for us one night. But please DO NOT try this at home with a blowtorch and DO NOT make this dish inside the house!

Serves 3

▌INGREDIENTS

3 beef tenderloin filets

2 tablespoons black peppercorns, coarsely ground

Pinch of coarse grey salt

1/4 cup cognac

1 cup heavy cream

Chopped chives for garnish

With a pepper grinder, on course, grind 2 tablespoons peppercorns and place on a small plate. Take each filet and press the peppercorns on the meat covering all sides and set aside on another plate. Sprinkle a pinch of the grey salt on each filet. Pan fry the steaks in a hot skillet on the burner of the grill to desired doneness, about 6-8 minutes per side depending on thickness. Remove the steaks to a platter and **turn off the burner to the grill.**

Lifting the skillet off the burner and **turning away from the grill,** add the cognac and then set to flame. When the flame burns out, turn the grill burner back on and place the skillet back on the heat. Then, add the cream and mix well. Return the steaks back to the pan and spoon the sauce over. Sprinkle with fresh chopped chives and serve.

MEDITERRANEAN STYLE GREEK OLIVE OIL POACHED STRIPED BASS WITH GARDEN HERBS AND LEMON

We are a fishing family and I'm lucky my husband and sons head to Connecticut almost every year and bring me back some sweet bass! Calvin caught several beauties one year. My friend Norma also gifted me the fish poacher I use in this recipe. It took me years to use it because it wouldn't fit in my oven. I was so excited to finally be able to use it, but if you don't have one, use any casserole dish just large enough to hold the fish.

*Serves 6 or 4 with leftovers for **striped bass burgers***

▌ INGREDIENTS

2 1/2 pound fillet of striped bass with the skin on

1 liter 33.8 ounces bottle Greek olive oil, here Bellucci from Mylopotamos, or any Greek olive oil, see **note**

1 lemon, thinly sliced

4 sprigs Italian oregano

4 sprigs golden oregano

2 basil tops

2 rosemary sprigs

4 garlic cloves, smashed

Salt mix

Freshly ground black pepper

Preheat oven to 250°F. Sprinkle fish with **1 1/2** teaspoons salt and a fresh grind of black pepper. Line the bottom tray of your poacher or casserole dish by alternating **1/2** of the lemon slices. Top with the fish fillet, skin side down. Lay the rest of the lemon slices on top of the fish. Add in the smashed cloves and herbs. Cover with the olive oil. Sprinkle a small pinch of salt and some freshly ground black pepper. See **photo** on page 327.

Poach exactly **1 1/2** hours for a **2 1/2** pound fillet. If your fillet is smaller or larger adjust the cooking time. As well, if using a heavier casserole pan, cooking time may be a little longer. When done, lift and drain the oil from the fish and place on a serving platter. Garnish with fresh lemon wedges and herbs and serve with any ripe sliced tomatoes. Sprinkle on some chive flowers if you have some and serve with a small bowl of the olive oil alongside from cooking to drizzle over the tomatoes, if desired. We love this with the **sautéed lambs quarters.**

Note: I am lucky to live in an area where I have so many specialty markets for all the cuisines I like to make, and once every 6 months or so, I make the rounds and stock up on ingredients. If you can't get a hold of Greek olive oil, try a nice Italian or Spanish olive oil. Striped bass is also called striper and rockfish, but you could also substitute halibut.

STRIPED BASS BURGERS

Fish burgers, or cakes as we also call them make the best blank canvas as you can add anything you like and use most any kind of fish. I have a ton of recipes for them but this is a favorite after the boys have been fishing and bring home some sweet fillets. You may adjust the ingredients depending on how many cups of flaked fish you have leftover, and of course, you may just cook the fish just to make these.

Serves 8 or 4 hungry, makes 8 burgers

▍INGREDIENTS

5 cups flaked, leftover baked striped bass from a 3 pound fillet, or from the Mediterranean Greek poached striper, may have 3 cups flaked here - be sure to add the gel and juice from the lemon slices from cooking the fish

1 medium red onion, diced fine (sometimes I like to use a bunch of scallions)

3 garlic cloves, minced

1 tablespoon extra-virgin olive oil

Sauté the onion and garlic in the olive oil about 10 minutes until translucent, but not brown. When done, set aside to cool. Meanwhile prepare other ingredients and lightly spray a baking sheet to set the burgers on for baking.

IN LARGE BOWL, ADD THE FOLLOWING

▌ I N G R E D I E N T S

Flaked striped bass

1/2 cup fresh parsley, minced
(a mix of basil and cilantro is
also delicious)

1/2 tablespoon Herbes de
Provence

1/2-3/4 teaspoon grey salt and
alder smoked salt mixed, or
just all grey salt

Freshly ground black pepper

Juice of 1/2-1 lemon, plus zest,
if desired

1 1/2 tablespoons capers,
minced

2 eggs blended

1 cup *gluten-free panko
breadcrumbs,* or *gluten-
free Italian style panko,* or
any breadcrumbs

1 Thai pepper minced, or
any minced hot pepper,
optional

Preheat oven to 425°F. Mix well and add more lemon juice if needed. Stir in the cooled onions and garlic. Mix again and using a **1/2** cup measurer, lightly sprayed so patty comes out easy, scoop up amount and then with your hands, form into a nicely shaped patty. (If I use 3 cups flaked fish, I use **1/3** cup measurer and it makes 6 patties.)

Place all on the prepared baking sheet and spray lightly the tops. Sprinkle just a touch of breadcrumbs on top if you have some left. Bake for 20 minutes. Alternately, pan fry until golden on each side using a non-stick skillet or well-seasoned cast iron pan so they don't stick.

SERVING SUGGESTIONS

Red leaf lettuce or mustard
greens for wraps

Sliced cucumbers

Tomato and avocado slices

Buns

Chopped basil or parsley

Lemon wedges

When the burgers are done, remove to a platter and serve with red leaf lettuce wraps, or mustard greens, two leaves per burger, or your favorite buns. If choosing lettuce, place thinly sliced cucumber tops on the lettuce, then the burger, and top with the sauce, parsley or basil, and lemon wedges. Add tomato and avocado slices, if desired. Serve with the **caper basil mayonnaise** or **Genovese basil and Vietnamese coriander aioli.**

CEDAR PAPER GRILLED SALMON WITH PEA PESTO AND HERBS

We all love salmon grilled on a cedar plank, but this is a fun way to serve them individually.
Serves 6-8

▌ INGREDIENTS

2-1 1/2 pound wild copper river sockeye salmon fillets, skin and pin bones removed (your fish guy will do this if you ask, but I keep tweezers in my kitchen just for this purpose), cut crosswise into 2 1/2-3-inch fillets

8 cedar papers, soaked at least one hour

8 pieces kitchen string, rinsed in water and excess water squeezed out

Juice of 1/2 to 1 lemon to drizzle over the top of the salmon

Salt mix

Freshly ground black pepper

Lemon wedges for serving

After papers have soaked, lay them on a work surface and place a salmon fillet vertical following the lines of the cedar paper. Drizzle with lemon juice and sprinkle with salt and pepper. Roll cedar paper around salmon and secure with the string, cutting off excess.

Grill on low, topside down first for 5 minutes. Flip and cook another 4-5 minutes. Take off the grill and let the wraps rest for 5 minutes. Cut the strings and tear the sides of the cedar wraps along the sides of the salmon, and serve the salmon directly on the cedar wrap. Serve with lemon wedges or with the **lemon cream dressing** and pea pesto with herbs, and mortar and pestle **basil pesto bruschetta,** or **roasted tomatoes bruschetta,** if desired.

PEA PESTO AND HERBS

This is served raw and goes great with the salmon. I make a ton because I like the extra for a great day-time snack or appetizer dip with your favorite cracker, but you could cut this recipe in half.

Serves 8-10

▌ INGREDIENTS

2 10-ounce bags frozen sweet peas, defrosted, quick rinsed and drained

2-3 small garlic cloves

1/2 cup Genovese basil and mint, mixed, chopped

1/4 teaspoon rosemary, minced

1/2 cup Pecorino Romano cheese, finely grated

1/3 cup olive oil

1/4 cup toasted pine nuts, cooled

1/2-1 teaspoon salt mix

Freshly ground black pepper

Add the peas and garlic to a food processor and pulse to blend. Add the herbs, cheese, olive oil, pine nuts, **1/2** teaspoon salt to start (the cheese is salty) and pepper. Pulse blend again leaving a nice texture.

Taste for seasoning, adding more salt if necessary. Form quenelles using 2 spoons to create the egg shape, if desired and serve with the salmon.

SKUNA BAY
BAKED SALMON

We absolutely love salmon and nowadays it's a treat more than a weekly staple. Substitute any wild salmon such as king, which is also a favorite.

Serves 2 with leftovers for the Skuna bay salmon cakes or will serve 4 without leftovers.

▌ INGREDIENTS

2 1/2 pounds center cut Skuna Bay salmon

Your best extra-virgin olive oil

1 lemon thinly sliced, seeds removed

Red Hawaiian sea salt, or coarse grey sea salt

Freshly ground black pepper

Preheat oven at 350°F. Place the salmon on a parchment lined baking sheet and drizzle a bit of oil over the top and rub all over the salmon. Again, pour the oil on a spoon and then use the back of the spoon to rub the oil around the salmon.

Sprinkle with the salt and pepper and lay the lemon slices over the top. Drizzle with a little more oil and bake for 12 minutes or so. You do not want to overcook the fish as it will dry out. It will also continue to cook once you take it out of the oven. Remove to a serving plate and let rest about 5 minutes.

SKUNA BAY
SALMON CAKES

If you do happen to have some leftover salmon, try making these.

Makes 6 cakes

▌ INGREDIENTS

2-3 tablespoons of extra virgin olive oil

1/2 medium onion, diced fine

3 garlic cloves, minced

1 tablespoon parsley stalks, minced

Freshly ground black pepper

3 cups flaked Skuna Bay salmon, or King salmon (save reserved gel from baking and add that plus the juice from the lemon slices)

1 tablespoon chives, minced

1 tablespoon parsley, minced

1/2 cup **gluten-free panko breadcrumbs**, or any breadcrumbs

1 egg blended

Salt mix

Freshly ground black pepper

In a medium non-stick skillet, add a drizzle of the olive oil and on medium heat, sauté the onions, garlic and parsley stalks with a pinch of salt and freshly ground black pepper until translucent and just beginning to brown a little. Remove from the heat and let cool. In a medium bowl, add the flaked salmon with any of the reserved gel and squeeze the remainder of the juice from any lemon slices left over.

Continue to add in the, chives, parsley, panko, the blended egg and pepper and mix well. Then add in the cooled onion mixture and mix well. Using **1/2** cup measure to portion, scoop the salmon and then with your hands, form into a nice cake. Drizzle the oil into the same skillet you used to sauté the onions and cook the cakes just below medium heat, about 8 minutes per side. Serve on your favorite bun or on a few leaves of your favorite lettuce with the **lemon chive mayonnaise**, **caper basil mayonnaise** or even the **cabin tartar sauce.**

BATTERED CRISPY "NORVERN" FOR TACOS, TOSTADAS OR NACHO BITES

My husband's family has an Island in Sioux Narrows, Canada, and the kids have been going since they were little. We call Northern Pike "norvern" and we love it and freeze plenty to bring home to enjoy the taste of fresh caught fish long after summer is over.

Serves 4

FOR THE BATTER

Make ahead and let sit aside an hour or more before cooking.

▌ INGREDIENTS

1 cup gluten-free flour, Bob's red mill 1 to 1 baking flour, or any flour

1 cup gluten-free beer (I like Red Bridge), adding more by 1/8 cup if necessary to get to consistency of drizzled pancake batter, or any beer

1 teaspoon garlic powder

1/2 teaspoon smoked paprika

1/2 teaspoon medium heat chili powder

1 teaspoon salt mix

Freshly ground black pepper

Taco shells, corn tortillas for tostadas, or nacho chips for whatever you choose to serve

Mix all ingredients except the taco shells, corn tortillas and nacho chips into a glass bowl and set aside, adding more beer if necessary to get to drizzled pancake batter consistency.

FOR COOKING

▌ INGREDIENTS

4 fillets northern pike cut into 16
　　pieces

Grapeseed oil for pan frying

Preheat oven to 275-300°F to keep the fish warm until all
are cooked. Gently cut each fillet in half crosswise pulling
out the long Y bones. Then, cut each half into 2 lengthwise
pieces being careful to remove the bones (northern pike
has a ton of bones but most long enough to pull out). This
makes 16 pieces.

Have some paper towels laid out for dabbing off the oil
when the fish is cooked and a baking sheet lined with
parchment to keep the fish warm until all are done.

In a large non-stick skillet, add a drizzle of grapeseed oil to
lightly coat the bottom of the pan. When pan is medium to
medium high, dip each piece of fish into the batter, dripping off excess and carefully add to the pan. Do not crowd
the pan and cook until golden, only turning once. When
done, with tongs, take out each piece and dab excess oil
on a paper towel and lay directly on the baking sheet.
Keep warm in the oven until all are done. You may need to
wipe the pan out and add new oil here and there.

continued ⟶

SUGGESTIONS FOR CONDIMENTS

Mix each and add into individual bowls to serve alongside your meal.

INGREDIENTS

Purple cabbage slaw, thinly sliced, squeeze of lime juice, pinch of cumin, cilantro, pinch salt mix

Sautéed red bell pepper and onion

Chopped greens drizzled with lime juice

Any fresh tomatoes, seeded and cubed with a little diced onion and lime juice

Refried **pinto beans for a crowd** or **easy weeknight pinto beans**

Cumin lime crema

Fresh garden tomatillo salsa

Guacamole

Chopped cilantro

Lime wedges

Build whatever you choose to serve with the fish. If serving tacos or nacho bites, I put everything on the table and let everyone add in what they like. If making tostadas, follow the directions for pan frying the corn tortillas for **tostadas**. Once the tortillas are ready, I like to spread with guacamole, layer on peppers and onions, add the fish, then top with the fresh garden tomatillo salsa and a spoonful of the tomatoes. Garnish with cilantro and serve with a lime wedge.

CRISPIEST BATTERED BASS AND "NORVERN" WITH CABIN TARTAR SAUCE

Serve this with the cabin tartar sauce and lemon wedges and go directly to heaven.

Serves 4

FOR THE CRISPIEST BATTER

🚩 INGREDIENTS

1 cup white rice flour

1 teaspoon red Alea Hawaiian
   fine grind salt, or grey salt

Freshly ground black pepper

1 bottle club soda – 1 cup, plus
   1/4 cup to pancake batter
   consistency

In a medium bowl, add the flour, salt, and pepper. Add one cup of the club soda and mix well. Let sit a few minutes as it will thicken. Then add **1/4** cup more club soda until batter is pancake consistency. Drizzle in a little more if necessary.

FOR THE FISH

🚩 INGREDIENTS

4-6 halves bass or northern
   fish, or a combination of
   both

Kerrygold butter and
   grapeseed oil for pan frying

In a non-stick skillet, add a drizzle of grapeseed oil and a pat of butter to lightly coat the bottom of the pan. When pan is medium high, dip each piece of fish into the batter and carefully add to the pan. Do not crowd the pan. Cook until golden only turning once. If the pan seems to be getting too hot, turn the heat down a notch. When done, with tongs, take out and transfer to a platter and serve with the tartar sauce and lemon wedges.

CABIN TARTAR SAUCE

For cabin bass, norvern, walleye, or any of your favorite fish or fish cake. This is the "Mac Daddy" of tartar sauces. I always bring my own mayonnaise to Canada, plus a jar of my pickled peppers, and a bag of fresh peppers so I'm well-armed for making my tartar sauce!

⚑ INGREDIENTS

1 1/2 cups mayonnaise, no need to measure

2-3 teaspoons Dijon mustard

squeeze of lemon and lime juice

parsley, basil or dill, chopped, about 1/4 cup

1 garlic clove, minced or grated

spoonful of capers, about 2 tablespoons, chopped

4 cornichon pickles chopped or 1 large dill pickle, chopped

2 tablespoons small red onion or sweet onion, diced

1 tablespoon pickled peppers, chopped with a spoonful or two of the juice, or 1 fresh hot pepper, seeded and minced (you could also use dill pickle juice)

In a medium bowl, mix all ingredients together and taste for seasoning. May need a pinch salt and black pepper or more lemon juice. Keep in the fridge for when the fish is ready to serve.

SKILLET HASH BROWNS
AND FRIED EGGS WITH GARDEN GREENS

This one pan dish is great anytime, makes for easy cleanup and sometimes eggs are just what you need for dinner.

Serves 2 – made for 2 but I only eat 1 egg

INGREDIENTS

1/2 medium-large sweet onion, diced

2 tablespoons Kerrygold butter, plus more for adding as potatoes cook

1/2 teaspoon hot smoked paprika, or sweet if you prefer

2 tablespoons cilantro stalks, minced

4 medium golden potatoes, peeled and cut 1/2 inch dice, or smaller cubes, about 4 cups, pat dry with paper towels after cutting

Pinch salt mix to taste

Freshly ground black pepper

5-6 smaller lacinato kale leaves, stalks removed, sliced chiffonade

8-10 baby tatsoi greens, sliced chiffonade

2 basil tops, about 12 leaves, sliced chiffonade

Cilantro to garnish

3 eggs (or you could do 4 - 2 per person)

3/4 cup Monterey Jack cheese.

In a large non-stick skillet, melt 2 tablespoons of the butter and add the onions and cilantro stalks. If you are not a fan of cilantro, substitute with parsley stalks or omit altogether. Sauté about 5-7 minutes then spread to outer edges of the pan. Add another tablespoon or so of butter and add potatoes, salt, pepper, and paprika. Lower the heat a little so the potatoes can cook through and brown, but not burn before being done, stirring every now and again, about 30 minutes. Add little bits of butter as necessary and continue to flip potatoes and onions to brown evenly.

Add the kale, tatsoi and basil. Mix in with the potatoes and at this point taste test a potato to make sure they are done. If al dente (firm to the bite), cook 5-7 minutes more. When all are done and golden, make 3 or 4 circles, moving potatoes to the sides as the border. Crack each egg in a small bowl and add one per spot. Cook at the same heat for 3 minutes. Sprinkle with salt and pepper, then add on 3/4 cup of the grated Monterey Jack cheese. Cover pan to melt the cheese, about 2-3 minutes more. Eggs should be done with a runny yolk, but if you like them more firm, cook a little longer. Sprinkle with cilantro and serve straight from the pan, because more often than not, when you want eggs for dinner, you don't want much to clean up either.

LEMON PASTA REQUEST

When the kids were little they loved this lemon pasta with a shape called campanelle. I have more recipes and variations on this over the years per the many requests of my daughter and sons who have asked me to make it, and if I'm making it, they will take any shape pasta!

Serves 4-6

INGREDIENTS

6 Italian sausages, half sweet and half spicy, see **note**

16 ounces spiral pasta, see note on next page for gluten-free pasta cooking time

1 1/2-2 cups finely grated Parmigiano-Reggiano cheese

1/4 cup chicken broth

1/4 cup half and half, optional, or use 1/2 cup chicken broth

2 garlic cloves, minced

1/2 cup lemon juice

1 cup basil, chopped (or a combo of basil, dill, parsley and chives)

For the sausage, you can either remove the casings and break up the sausage meat as you sauté until just nice and brown, and then drain the grease, or you may slice the sausage into about one inch rounds, cooking until just brown. We love either way and it depends what you're in the mood for.

When done cooking, set the sausage aside and wipe the grease out of the pan. Add the minced garlic and stir about half a minute. Then add the chicken broth and half and half, if using, to deglaze the pan, stirring with a wooden spoon to get up all the brown bits.

Meanwhile in a large pot of boiling salted water, cook your pasta to al dente (firm to the bite), drain and add to a large serving bowl. Pour the pan sauce over the pasta and add in the cooked sausage, lemon juice and about **11/4** cups cheese, saving the rest to pass along on the side. Taste for seasoning. Sprinkle with some freshly ground black pepper and the basil.

Note: Use whatever protein you like or leave it out entirely. We love the sausage above as whenever my father Francis visited, he used to bring it to me homemade by his buddy from Springfield, MA. Since his passing, my brother Fran now brings me some every time he comes for a visit. Hot Italian chicken sausage is also nice here. Leftover flaked king salmon is also a big winner and you can't go wrong tossing in some ripe juicy tomatoes.

PENNE WITH SAUSAGE AND TOMATO WITH LAMBS QUARTERS AND HOLY BASIL PESTO

This makes such a quick and easy meal with pesto from the freezer, especially if you have nighttime school functions to go to. I happened to make this a few years ago on my last ever high school back-to-school night for my son Nolan.

Serves 4 with leftovers for the lunchbox

INGREDIENTS

- 1 16-ounce bag penne pasta, Tinkyáda brand, see **note**

- 1 batch pesto of any kind, fresh or from the freezer, about 3/4-1 cup, see **lambs quarters and holy basil pesto**

- 6 sausages, any variety, here 3 chicken apple and 3 spinach feta

- 1 cup finely grated Parmigiano-Reggiano cheese

- 1 large Grampy Italian heirloom tomato, or any fresh ripe tomato

Cut the sausages into 1/2 inch coins. In a skillet, pan fry the sausages until nicely browned on both sides and cooked through. When sausages are halfway cooked, heat up the water for the pasta. When boiling, add about a tablespoon of salt and add the pasta. Stir around to keep from sticking. Continue to cook the pasta and when done, reserve about 1/2 cup pasta water, then drain, and return to the cooking pot.

Stir in the pesto to your desired amount and a spoonful or two of the reserved pasta water. When sausages are fully cooked, drain on a paper towel and then add to the pasta. Toss in 1 cup grated Parmigiano cheese and mix well. Turn onto a large serving platter or save on cleanup and serve right out of the pot. Dice up one large tomato and sprinkle over the pasta. Sprinkle another grating of Parmigiano cheese and grind of black pepper and serve.

Note: We love the Tinkyáda brand for an organic brown rice gluten-free pasta. However, I absolutely do not cook according to package directions or the pasta would be mush. Add salt into the boiling water and cook 10-11 minutes and drain. If I'm doing a casserole and baking after, I cook for 8 minutes. But always give a taste test so it doesn't get overcooked.

NO BAKE GARDEN CUCUMBER AND TOMATO LASAGNA WITH ITALIAN PINE NUT SPREAD AND BASIL MINT PESTO

This raw vegan dish makes the most of fresh vegetables at their peak. This recipe has a few steps but comes together easily if you make the Italian pine nut spread and the basil mint pesto the day before.

ITALIAN PINE NUT SPREAD

*I love soaking nuts for dips. See **note**. This has an unbelievable similarity in consistency to ricotta cheese – even my husband didn't believe me when I told him it was pine nuts!*

▌INGREDIENTS

2 cups raw pine nuts soaked in a bowl of water for 2-4 hours. (The longer they soak, the lighter the spread; 4 hours is preferable. Reserve 1/4 cup of the soaked nuts for the basil mint pesto.)

5 tablespoons water

2 1/2 tablespoons lemon juice and zest

1/2 teaspoon salt mix

Drain the pine nuts and place ingredients in a food processor starting with 3 tablespoons of water and pulse to blend. Scrape sides of the bowl, pulse blending until fluffy, adding more water one tablespoon at a time if needed to achieve a creamy consistency. I find if the nuts are soaked longer than 3 hours, they need less water when blending. Taste for seasoning and cover and keep in the refrigerator until ready to use. See **photo** on page 330.

Note: To make the pine nut spread to serve as a hors d'oeuvre spread, make as above, then also add in one minced clove of garlic, any hot pepper of choice, seeded and minced, and any of your favorite herbs. Taste for seasoning and serve with breadsticks, toasted baguette slices or any cracker.

BASIL MINT PESTO

Feel free to substitute any of the pestos in this book, but to keep it vegan friendly, this one uses the soaked pine nuts as a stand in for the traditional Parmigiano-Reggiano cheese.

▌INGREDIENTS

2 cups packed Genovese basil

1 cup packed mint

1/3 cup – 1/2 cup olive oil

2 garlic cloves

1/4 cup of the soaked pine nuts, reserved from the *Italian pine nut spread* before blending

1/4 teaspoon salt

Lots of fresh ground black pepper

Drain the soaked nuts. Add all ingredients to the food processor except the nuts and pulse blend with **1/3** cup olive oil to start. Sometimes, depending on how "packed" the herbs are, more may be needed to achieve pesto consistency. Add in the nuts and pulse blend adding the rest of the olive oil if necessary. Taste for seasoning and place in a glass container and set in the fridge until ready to prepare the lasagna.

LAYERING THE LASAGNA

▌INGREDIENTS

2-4 long cucumbers, or enough to make 12 thin 1/8 inch lengthwise slices – here, garden tokiwa cucumbers, or any long cucumbers, such as suyo long, or English to get strips without seeds

2 large heirloom tomatoes – here, 1 persimmon heirloom and 1 Andrew Rahart - use whatever is fresh and ripe, seeds removed if preferred, sliced thin and patted dry

1 batch *Italian pine nut spread*

1 batch *basil mint pesto*

Freshly ground black pepper

In a glass or enamel casserole about **6 1/2 x 9 1/2**, begin by layering the cucumber slices to cover the bottom slightly overlapping each one. With a spatula, gently spread a layer of the Italian pine nut spread and then a layer of basil mint pesto. Place the tomato slices alternating by color and slightly overlapping each one. Season with freshly ground black pepper, but no salt, as this will make the tomatoes release their juice and make the dish too watery.

Add another layer of the cucumber slices followed by another layer of the pine nut spread, and then the basil mint pesto. Arrange another layer of tomatoes and lattice any leftover cucumber slices on the top. Add some freshly ground black pepper.

This can be made ahead for about one hour and left to chill in the refrigerator. Any longer and it will become watery. It may also sit at room temperature for no longer than an hour. When ready to serve, using a very sharp knife, cut into squares taking care to gently lift a slice out of the casserole dish and transfer to the serving plate. Garnish with basil seed flowers and a drizzle of extra virgin olive oil with a pinch of salt, if desired.

Venetian Gondolier

OUT OF THIS WORLD *favorites*

Some of my greatest memories throughout my life have been associated with incredible food. So, I took great pleasure in sharing new foods with my kids as they grew up. We all have adventurous palettes and enjoy sampling new foods and flavors, so it is only natural for us to explore cultures and cuisines from our travels, and even restaurants back home, then return to the kitchen to replicate what we loved most.

SINGAPORE NOODLE

Back when we all started eating gluten free, it became increasingly hard to dine out or get takeout. There were only a couple restaurants that served some dishes that were gluten free and one favorite takeout dish we came to enjoy was Thai style Singapore noodle. The flavors were great, but the meat was always fatty, so I came up with this version so we could make whenever we wanted. This dish is easily made with any leftover meat.

▮ INGREDIENTS

FOR THE CURRY MIX

3 teaspoons sweet curry powder or 4 teaspoons if not using the Thai style

2 teaspoons Thai style curry powder

1 teaspoon hot curry powder

1/2-3/4 cup Thai basil leaves, washed and spun dry

Add first three ingredients to a small bowl and set the basil leaves aside in another bowl.

FOR THE PROTEINS

2 chicken breasts sliced lengthwise into thirds and then slice crosswise into 1/4 inch strips

3/4 pound ribeye steak, trimmed of fat and sliced thin

3/4 pounds cooked shrimp

2 tablespoons toasted sesame oil

2 tablespoons chili oil, or *spicy toasted sesame oil*

Salt mix and freshly ground black pepper to taste

In a large skillet, heat up 1 tablespoon sesame oil and 1 tablespoon chili oil and on medium heat, add the chicken, and sprinkle on some of the curry mix (You want to sprinkle on each of the protein steps so don't use it all here. Save some for onion mixture.) and cook until done. Transfer to a medium bowl and do the same for the steak. Season with salt and pepper. Add cooked shrimp and if the shrimp are not cooked, add just a drizzle of the sesame oil and cook until pink a few minutes per side. When all proteins are done place back in the skillet with their juices, cover and set aside.

FOR THE ONION MIX

1/2 large Vidalia onion cut lengthwise in half and then crosswise into thin slices

1 bunch scallions, sliced, saving some greens for garnish

3-4 Thai peppers minced, or more or less to your taste

Drizzle of toasted sesame oil and drizzle of olive oil

8 ounces mung bean sprouts, rinsed and drained

FOR THE PASTA

1 pound gluten-free thin spaghetti, Tinkyáda, or regular capellini

1-2 tablespoons toasted sesame oil

1 teaspoon curry powder, optional

Note: This recipe is easily made with leftover steak and chicken, 3 cups total plus added shrimp if you have it in the freezer (optional). Chives are also delicious if you have no scallions, just pick about 12 and cut into 2 inch pieces. And of course, you can add any hot peppers you like or leave them out entirely.

You can start cooking this mixture while the meat is cooking. In another skillet, sauté the onion, scallions, and Thai peppers in a drizzle of sesame oil and a drizzle of olive oil. Cook until translucent, about 15 minutes. Toss in the mung bean sprouts and sauté just a couple more minutes – you want them to retain their crispness. When done, add to the skillet of meats and shrimp. Keep warm and covered on a low burner while pasta cooks.

Cook the pasta in a large pot of boiling water with about a tablespoon of salt, about 10-11 minutes. See **note** with **penne with sausage**.

Drain the pasta and place in a large serving bowl. Drizzle with the sesame oil. Add the rest of the curry mix with another teaspoon of curry powder if desired. Toss well then add back the cooked meats, shrimp and the onion mixture. Add the fresh basil leaves and toss again. Serve with a side of minced Thai peppers for those who like it extra spicy.

THAI "PEACH" PAPAYA SALAD

This is a nice refreshing salad that we love ordering from our favorite Thai restaurant. Every time I would attempt replicating at home, my papaya had always ripened a little before I was able to make the salad. We've decided we like it even better with a papaya that has ripened a little, hence the "peach" color.

▌ INGREDIENTS

2 tablespoons fish sauce

1 tablespoon coconut palm sugar

Juice of 1 lime, at least 2 tablespoons or more to taste (salad should have a nice zing to it)

1 medium green papaya that has ripened a little so it is "peach" in color, but not too ripe or it would be too mushy to shred

Any garden tomato, seeded and chopped

6 green beans (I happened to have a few purple and green in the garden so I added those), each cut into thirds, optional

1 Thai pepper, minced

2 small garlic cloves, minced

1/2 cup or more cilantro, chopped

In a small bowl combine the fish sauce, palm sugar, and the lime juice. Mix well to dissolve the sugar and set aside while preparing the other ingredients.

Peel the papaya, cut in half lengthwise. Scoop out the seeds and shred using a mandolin, hand shredder (looks like a potato peeler), or cut into matchstick pieces by hand. Place papaya into a large bowl and add the beans, pepper, garlic and most of the cilantro saving some to sprinkle on top. Pour the sauce over and mix well topping with a little cilantro.

GENERAL TSO'S CHICKEN WINGS

Instead of the tiny pieces of chicken in inches of doughy greasy batter you get at the takeout place, I came up with this crispy version using the wings. Everyone loves these! Plus, it's gluten free so all can enjoy this Chinese classic!

*Serves 4-6 with the **Chinese style vegetable fried rice***

▌ INGREDIENTS

PREPARE THE CHICKEN

4 pounds split chicken wings (I like Bell & Evans Family pack 35-36 pieces)

1 teaspoon grey salt

1 teaspoon freshly ground black pepper

1/2 cup sake (you could use a Chinese wine such as Shaoxing, but I can get sake at my grocery store)

In a large non-reactive bowl, mix well with a spatula and refrigerate 2-4 hours flipping a few times.

PREPARE THE SAUCE

1 cup unsalted chicken broth

8 garlic cloves, minced

5 tablespoons local raw honey

5 tablespoons mirin (sweet rice cooking wine, or more sake if you don't have any)

5 tablespoons gluten-free tamari, low sodium soy sauce

5-6 tablespoons *vinegar red hot sauce*, or any vinegar based hot sauce

4 teaspoons tapioca starch

6 whole dried Asian peppers, optional

In a small bowl, add all ingredients except the Asian peppers and mix well and refrigerate until ready to cook the chicken. I like making this step ahead.

PREPARING TO COOK THE CHICKEN

Have a large bowl ready for tossing the chicken and sauce when chicken is done. (A large stainless steel bowl works well for tossing). Also, have a large shallow platter ready to go to fit the chicken and sauce for serving.

▌ INGREDIENTS

3 tablespoons baking powder (makes for crispy skin), plus extra if needed

3 tablespoons tapioca starch, plus extra if needed

Note: I have made this several times with 2 ovens, but only made with one oven when I cut the recipe in half using 2 pounds wings. If using one oven for 4 pounds, try putting the drumettes tray on the middle rack to start and the wings under that. Flip after the 15 minutes and put the wings on top for 10 minutes and take out. Then move the drumettes back to the middle rack for another 3-4 minutes. Or, just split the sauce in half and cook each separate for the allotted time.

Set oven to broil on HIGH. When ready to start cooking, remove the chicken from the fridge and let sit about 20 minutes to bring to room temperature. Then drain the chicken by holding a plate over the chicken, draining the liquid in the sink. Sprinkle the baking powder and tapioca starch directly onto the chicken and mix around well coating each piece to absorb any moisture. If chicken is still too moist, add another **1 1/2** tablespoons of tapioca starch.

On 2 large baking sheets lightly sprayed with coconut oil spray, add chicken, skin side down with enough space between each piece for air to circulate. I try to keep all the wing parts on one pan and the drumette parts on another because they take a little longer to cook. Place each pan on the middle rack using two ovens and broil for 15 minutes. Once the chicken goes in, add the sauce, and the dried Asian peppers if using, to a medium saucepan and bring to a low boil, then continue to simmer and stir until thickened, about 3 minutes. Keep sauce warm on low until chicken is done.

Take the wing pan out first and flip each one using tongs. Return to the oven and cook another 10 minutes. Take out the drumette pan and flip each of those and return to the oven for another 12-13 minutes, but it will vary depending the size of yours – the Bell and Evans ones are pretty meaty, just keep an eye out so they don't burn. (Alexa comes in handy for setting timers). When the chicken is done, add all to your large tossing bowl, pour the sauce over and toss well flipping with the bowl or a spatula. Place the chicken and sauce on a serving platter. I like spreading the chicken out on the platter versus stacking in a bowl, that way the chicken stays crispier. Sprinkle with chives, scallions, or cilantro if desired.

CHINESE STYLE VEGETABLE FRIED RICE

Whenever we get take out Thai, Chinese or Indian food, I always save the containers of plain white rice which makes it super easy to whip this up. You may use a large non-stick sauté pan or wok for this dish.

INGREDIENTS

4 cups cold white rice, or the **jasmine rice**

1 1/2 teaspoons coconut palm sugar

2-3 teaspoons grapeseed oil or refined coconut oil

1 small sweet onion, finely diced

Bunch of scallions at least 6, diced and save some for garnish

1 tablespoon fresh ginger, chopped

1 tablespoon garlic, minced

1/2 cup carrots, finely diced

3 eggs blended, set aside in a small bowl

3-5 tablespoons gluten-free tamari, low sodium soy sauce

Bring prepared rice of choice to room temperature. Flake the rice with a fork in a large bowl to separate then sprinkle with the sugar. Prepare all other ingredients so they are ready to add as needed.

In a large non-stick sauté pan, or wok, heat over medium to medium high heat depending on your cooktop. Add the oil and when hot, add the onion, scallions, garlic and ginger and stir fry about 5 minutes. Add the carrots and continue to stir fry, stirring around with a wooden spoon. Add the rice and continue to stir fry until mixed, then with your spoon, push all ingredients to the outer edge of the pan leaving a circle open in the middle. (If the pan temperature has gone down, turn up a notch.) Add in the blended eggs and let them cook. When starting to set, flip them around until cooked, and then mix well with the rice. Drizzle on the soy sauce, stir well, and continue cooking the rice. I like when some of the rice gets crispy and browned. Taste for seasoning. Turn out into a serving dish and sprinkle with the scallion slices.

Note: If making as a main dish, like a combination fried rice, feel free to add any leftover chicken, steak, pork, ham or shrimp. Add in with the carrots and add peas if you like them. May need an extra tablespoon of soy sauce.

OUR FAVORITE LEMONGRASS BEEF

We grow lemongrass in the garden and one year it spread so far we had the best harvest, but unfortunately, we also found that it dies in the winter. So, from then on, we grow it in a container and bring it inside through winter. This meal is a favorite celebration dish I always made when my sons finished a week of their music camp. Of course we make it anytime the craving strikes and anyone who tries this loves it!

Serves 6

▌ INGREDIENTS

4 pounds skirt steak, or boneless sirloin, trimmed of fat, sliced in 1 inch slices against the grain, see **note** on next page

4-5 lemongrass stalks, see **note**

4 large garlic cloves, minced

6 tablespoons fish sauce

6 tablespoons toasted sesame oil

4 tablespoons coconut palm sugar or packed light brown sugar

Juice of 1/2 lemon

A few chives or cilantro, chopped for garnish

In a large glass roasting pan, add the lemongrass, garlic, fish sauce, sesame oil, and palm sugar. Stir to mix and dissolve sugar with a fork. Prepare the beef and place in the marinade in one layer making sure all the slices are coated. Refrigerate until ready to grill, at least 4-6 hours, but best overnight. Occasionally, take out and flip the meat over so all is marinated well and remove from the fridge a half hour before grilling.

Grill slices over medium heat a few minutes per side or to your desired liking. Remove slices as they are done to a serving platter and keep warm and let the meat rest 5-10 minutes before serving. Sprinkle with the chives or cilantro, if desired.

Note: Lemongrass can be about **1 1/2** feet long, but you only use the bottom 4-5 inches. I bend it to see where it easily bends, then cut it off there. Then peel layers of the skin off revealing the nice smooth interior. Trim the root end and cut from the top leaving about 4-5 inches. Using a sharp knife, mince carefully – lemongrass is kind of tough. In a pinch, I've used the zest of 2 lemons, plus the juice from 1 when I wanted to make this dish but didn't have any lemongrass. It's not exactly the same flavor as lemongrass, but works well.

FOR THE ACCOMPANIMENTS

Serve with the following accompaniments on the side, if desired. I like to arrange all on a large serving platter so everyone can help themselves.

▌ INGREDIENTS

Scallions, white parts thinly sliced lengthwise

1/2-1 Japanese cucumber or English cucumber, peeled and thinly sliced

Large handful fresh mint leaves

Large handful fresh basil leaves, preferably Thai but any basil is fine

1 or 2 heads lettuce for wrapping the meat slices, such as bibb, Boston or your favorite lettuce

Small bowl of roasted peanuts or macadamia nuts, chopped, optional

Lime wedges

To serve, help yourselves to a lettuce leaf and place the meat and anything you want on top. Squeeze on a little lime juice, wrap it up and enjoy! Fantastic served with the **best ever cellophane noodles**, as the sauce for that is great drizzled over the meat. If not serving the noodles, make half the sauce for the meat if you wish. This meat is also great just gobbled up on its own and I serve it with anything.

Note: Most of the time I use skirt steak, also known as flap meat. Generally the meat is quite long, so I cut crosswise into 2 or 3 pieces, then take those pieces, turn and cut lengthwise across the grain.

BEST EVER CELLOPHANE NOODLES

*These noodles are awesome served with **our favorite lemongrass beef.** For a vegetarian dinner, serve with all the accompaniments to the beef to make lettuce wraps. This makes a ton so if you are serving 2-4 people, split the recipe in half. Best made the day of serving. If made ahead, bring to room temp before serving.*

Serves 6

INGREDIENTS

1 8-ounce package cellophane noodles, (also called mung bean noodles or bean thread, see *my cupboard*)

1 bunch of scallions, sliced in half lengthwise and then sliced thinly on the bias crosswise

1 cup cilantro, chopped

Large handful arugula, chopped, or 1 small head romaine lettuce, sliced thinly crosswise

1 carrot, thinly sliced matchstick or shredded

3-4 tablespoons toasted sesame oil

FOR THE SAUCE

1/4 cup fish sauce

Scant half cup water

1 tablespoon brown sugar or about 1 1/2 tablespoons coconut palm sugar

3-4 tablespoons lime juice

1-2 sliced Thai bird chilis, or as many as you like depending on how spicy you like it

Bring a medium saucepan of water to a boil, add noodles, turn the heat to a gentle simmer and stir with a fork as they cook about 10 minutes. They will become clear and see through. Turn noodles out into a fine mesh strainer and set that over the saucepan, off heat to let the noodles drain well, about 20-30 minutes.

Meanwhile, in a medium nonreactive bowl, add the sauce ingredients and set aside stirring occasionally to dissolve the sugar.

Prepare the other ingredients for the noodles and place in a bowl. When the noodles have drained well, add them to a large serving bowl. Drizzle with the toasted sesame oil. Using a sharp knife and fork, slice the noodles about 3 times in each direction to make the noodles smaller and easier to eat. Add the other ingredients from the bowl and with two large spoons, toss well. Spoon about half the sauce over and toss well. Add more sauce if needed, otherwise, serve alongside for those who like more, or if serving alongside the lemongrass beef.

FALAFEL WITH TAHINI AND CILANTRO SAUCE

Whenever I soak chickpeas for hummus, I save enough to make this dish. It's a special treat and they also make a great cocktail hour nibble.

▌ INGREDIENTS

2 1/4 cups dry chickpeas, soaked in filtered water at least 20-24 hours, rinsing water occasionally and keep bowl covered in the fridge, see **note**

1 small sweet or yellow onion, cut in eighths

1/2 cup packed parsley

1/2 cup packed cilantro

2 garlic cloves, minced

1 1/2 teaspoons ground cumin

1 1/2 teaspoons baking powder, or baking soda

1 teaspoon ground coriander

1 teaspoon salt mix

1/4 teaspoon ground cayenne

Grapeseed oil or olive oil for pan frying

In a large food processor, add all ingredients except the oil and pulse blend scraping down sides to form a coarse mixture (not chunky, but don't want to blend so much it becomes hummus). Scrape down sides again and pulse blend to the right consistency. Add all to a bowl and set in the refrigerator about 30 minutes (can also be made ahead).

On a baking tray lined with parchment, use a 1 inch scoop or a 1/4 cup measure to form balls and pat into patties. Place on the parchment. When all are done, if you are ready to pan fry go ahead, otherwise, cover with another sheet of parchment and place in the fridge until ready to cook. I usually make them ahead so when I'm ready to cook I can just grab them and they are ready to go.

In a large non-stick skillet, add a layer of oil just to cover the bottom of the pan. Cook on medium, flipping once to brown on both sides. If the patty is sticking, it is not ready to turn, so if you think it is going to burn and still won't turn, bring down the heat a little, but you don't want the falafel soaking up the oil on too low heat, about 5-8 minutes. Turn gently and brown the other side, about 5 minutes more. Drain on paper towels and serve with the tahini sauce and cilantro sauce.

Note: After chickpeas have been soaked and rinsed, they keep well covered in the fridge a few days before making the falafel – they may even sprout! Just be sure to rinse and drain them.

FOR THE TAHINI SAUCE

▌INGREDIENTS

1 cup tahini paste or raw tahini
paste

1/3 cup lemon juice, or more to
taste and zest if you like

2 garlic cloves, minced

1/2-3/4 cups filtered water,
starting with 1/2 cup, then
add by 1/4 cup at a time to get
to the sauce consistency

1/2-1 teaspoon salt to taste

In a small food processor, add the tahini, lemon juice
and garlic to blend. You will see after you add the lemon
juice, suddenly the tahini gets extremely thick. It is at this
point to start adding the water. We love a lot of lemon
juice. Taste as you go along perhaps adding more lemon
juice if you like along with water.

FOR THE CILANTRO SAUCE

▌INGREDIENTS

1 cup packed cilantro including
stems

1 green hot pepper, cayenne or
jalapeño, optional

1 tablespoon lemon juice, plus
more to taste

1 tablespoon orange juice

1 1/2 tablespoons sour cream,
or for dairy free, substitute
coconut cream from a can

Pinch ground cumin

Pinch salt mix

In a high-speed blender, add all ingredients and blend
well. Taste for seasoning and adjust to your taste. We like
it spicy!

PERUVIAN LOMO SALTADO

I have been growing Peruvian peppers for so many years and especially love making Amarillo sauce, but it wasn't until my husband and daughter planned a trip to Peru that I got pumped up to make this staple Peruvian dish. I considered leaving out the French fries, but sure was glad I didn't because they make the dish along with the amazing gravy. You could certainly make your own French fries for this dish, but I find Alexia Yukon gold select work perfectly. I also like the Alexia steak fries because they hold up nicely with the gravy. It takes about 20 minutes to cook up the following ingredients. Check your package directions on the cooking time for your French fries to plan that they are done at the same time the meat mixture is done.

Serves 2

▌ INGREDIENTS

1 8-ounce filet mignon, or your favorite steak

Olive oil for cooking

5 small to medium garden variety tomatoes, cut in half or bigger ones in quarters, seeded

2 red Cipollini onions or 1 medium red onion, sliced in half and then cut into slices

2 garlic cloves, minced

2-3 tablespoons *ají Amarillo sauce*, see resources

1 ají Amarillo pepper, seeded, cut into slices crosswise

1/2 teaspoon ground cumin

1/2 teaspoon ground epazote, or known as Paico in Peru, see *note*, optional

1/4 cup gluten-free soy sauce, low sodium, plus enough water to make 1/3 cup

1 tablespoon fresh mint, chopped

1/2 cup fresh cilantro, chopped, reserving some for garnish

Slice filet into **1/4** inch slices and season with freshly ground black pepper, **1/4** teaspoon of the cumin and **1/4** teaspoon of the epazote. (I do not salt the meat because the soy sauce added later provides the salt – otherwise it would be too salty.) In a medium skillet (I like my cast iron for this.), add a drizzle of the oil and cook beef on medium heat until just done and browned. Remove and set aside in a bowl.

In the same skillet, add the onions, Amarillo pepper, and the garlic, adding a dash more oil if you need it. When onions are soft and translucent, add in the Amarillo sauce and stir around to mix. Add the beef back into the skillet along with the soy sauce and water. Add in the tomatoes, the other **1/4** teaspoon cumin and **1/4** teaspoon epazote, mint, cilantro, and mix well. The fries should be done, or close to being done, and the beef mixture can stay warm a few minutes if the fries need a little more time. For serving, put some French fries on the plate and top with a big scoop of the meat and tomatoes. Add a few more fries and top with more goodies being sure to get some sauce. Sprinkle on the mint and reserved cilantro and serve.

Note: I planted epazote one time years ago and have never had to plant it again. It comes up volunteer in many containers on the patio and sometimes I find it in the garden. See note on drying herbs in the **miscellaneous** section.

CROCK POT TACO MEAT

This is a version of my mom Marilyn's famous taco meat, but here I use the crock pot. Absolutely the best for virtually any Mexican dish.

▌ INGREDIENTS

3 pounds grass-fed boneless beef chuck roast, or chuck shoulder

1 large white or yellow onion, diced

6-8 large garlic cloves, roughly chopped

1 can large pitted black olives, sliced, reserve the juice

1/2 of a 4 ounce can mild or hot diced green chilis, save the other half for the pinto beans, if making, optional

1 tablespoon Mexican oregano

2 teaspoons dried epazote, optional

1 tablespoon chili powder (sometimes I use 1/2 tablespoon chipotle chili powder and 1/2 tablespoon ancho chili powder)

1/2 tablespoon ground coriander

1 teaspoon ground cumin

3/4 teaspoon salt mix

Freshly ground black pepper

Preheat the crock pot on high while preparing the beef and set the timer for **8 1/2 hours**. Spread the diced onion on the bottom of the pot. Trim beef of fat and cut into 2-3 inch cubes and then spread over the top of the onions. Top with the sliced olives, garlic and mild chilis, if using. Pour one cup of olive juice over top and cover for 2 hours.

Add the seasonings and stir to mix well. Stir periodically over the next **6-6 1/2 hours** and skim fat with a spoon. At the 5-6 hour mark, try breaking up the meat with a wooden spoon when you stir. I often drain the condensation on the lid onto a towel each time I stir, especially if I see too much liquid accumulating. If there is too much liquid, take the top off for an hour or so before the end of cooking time, but don't let it all evaporate because when you shred the meat, the liquid soaks right in. The meat should break up easily with your wooden spoon or help it along shredding with 2 forks.

Epazote

EASY WEEKNIGHT PINTO BEANS

*I love making **pinto beans for a crowd (see next page)**. They are great to have on hand for a party, or when I know all the kids are coming home, I'll whip some up to portion and freeze. This makes for an easy fiesta or quick weeknight meals. But, I also fall back on these quite a bit when serving a last minute Mexican meal. Feel free to substitute black beans.*

Serves 4-5 alongside a Mexican meal, makes enough for 8 tostadas

INGREDIENTS

1 tablespoon olive oil or grapeseed

1 25-ounce can pinto beans, rinsed and drained

1 medium onion, finely diced

2 cloves garlic, minced

1 jalapeño pepper, seeded and minced, or 1 4-ounce can mild or hot diced green chilis

1/3-1/2 cup chicken broth (Or, I also use olive juice from a can of black or green olives if I am incorporating olives into the meal.)

Juice of 1/2 lime, or more to taste

1 teaspoon ground cumin

Salt mix to taste, about 1/2 teaspoon

Freshly ground black pepper

2 tablespoons cilantro, chopped

Heat the oil in a medium saucepan and on medium heat, add the onions and jalapeño (or chilis), and sauté about 10 minutes. Add in the garlic and sauté a few minutes more. Stir in the beans, **1/3** cup chicken broth to start (or olive juice), and the lime juice. Cook stirring on medium and with the back of a wooden spoon, start mashing the beans as they soften.

Add in the cumin, salt to taste and freshly ground black pepper. Stir, reducing heat as beans get creamier so they don't stick to the bottom of the pan. Taste for seasoning, adding more broth, lime juice, or salt, if necessary, and stir in the cilantro. Cover and keep warm on low heat until ready to serve your meal, or let cool a bit before spreading as the first layer on a tostada.

PINTO BEANS
FOR A CROWD

These beans are so versatile, and they may be prepared ahead and frozen, making it easy to put together a Mexican fiesta. I usually double this using two pounds beans, but here I use one pound. Just note that the beans require soaking and I prefer 2 days over one. Do not be tempted to salt the beans while they are cooking because it makes the skins hard.

FOR THE BEANS

▌ INGREDIENTS

1 pound pinto beans, picked through for small stones and removing damaged and split beans

Rinse the beans in a colander and place in a large bowl. Cover with about 4-5 inches water, as beans will expand. Cover beans with plastic wrap and leave on the counter out of direct light. After a day, drain water and rinse, then cover with fresh water and soak until ready to cook the next day. I usually put mine to soak on a Friday night or Saturday morning and cook them up on Sunday.

When ready to cook the beans, drain water and rinse them well and add to the cooking pot. Add 8 cups water or enough to cover beans by one inch of water. Bring to a boil and skim the froth as it comes up. Turn the heat to a medium simmer, about **2–2 1/2** hours, uncovered. Stir often so beans don't stick, continuing to skim off any froth that comes up. Once froth subsides keep the lid tilted.

After about **1 1/2** hours, taste a bean and if it is starting to soften, you may start to mash them a little with a wooden spoon or a potato masher. As time goes on, mash some more leaving some beans whole. It may seem like there is a lot of liquid, but as beans are mashed, they will absorb more liquid and generally they come out nice and creamy, but if you need a little more water, add by **1/4** cup. As the beans come closer to being done, stir more often and turn the heat a notch or two lower because the creamier they get, the easier they stick to the bottom of the pan.

FOR THE ONION MIXTURE

⚑ INGREDIENTS

1 tablespoon olive oil

1 large onion, diced

1/2 of a 4 ounce can mild or hot diced green chilis, save the other half for the taco meat or use the entire can if you double this recipe

3 large garlic cloves, minced

1 jalapeño or serrano pepper, minced, optional

Salt mix

Freshly ground black pepper

Meanwhile, in a skillet, heat up the olive oil and add the onion, **1/2** can hot green chilies, the garlic cloves and jalapeño, seasoning with a pinch of salt and pepper. Sauté until soft and the onions are slightly browned, about 20 minutes.

FOR MIXING THE BEANS WITH THE ONION MIXTURE AND SEASONING

⚑ INGREDIENTS

2 teaspoons salt

Freshly ground black pepper

1 teaspoon ground cumin

1 teaspoon Mexican oregano

1 teaspoon chili powder, optional and any chili powder of choice

Juice of 1/2 lime

When beans are tender and done, and mashed to your liking, add 1 teaspoon salt, pepper, cumin, oregano, chili powder, and lime juice. Then stir the onion mixture into the beans. Taste for seasoning and add 1 more teaspoon salt. If more liquid is necessary, add **1/2** cup reserved olive juice (from the olives for the taco meat) or water.

Note: Use these beans for chip and dip, refried beans side dish, burritos and bowls, enchiladas, tostadas, or use in a layered Mexican dip. If freezing, let beans cool, then portion as you wish to containers.

MASTER TOMATILLO SAUCE FOR CHILAQUILES, ENCHILADAS, NACHOS, TACOS, OR TOSTADAS

Plant tomatillos once and you'll never have to plant them again! They come up volunteer every year and by the end of summer there are hundreds of them! I also see plenty at the farmer's market and grocery stores.

Makes about **4 1/2** *cups.*

▌ INGREDIENTS

2 pounds tomatillos, large ones halved for collecting seeds to save, if desired, plus enough water to cover tomatillos while cooking, reserving at least 1 cup liquid for blending

2 teaspoons extra virgin olive oil

3 large garlic cloves, whole

4 serrano peppers, halved and seeded, or jalapeño peppers

3/4 inch thick slices from a medium sized onion, about 4 slices

1/4 teaspoon grey salt

Juice of 1/2 lime

1/2 bunch cilantro with stalks

Peel and rinse the tomatillos (they will feel sticky). Add to a medium stock pot and cover with water. Bring to a low boil and continue boiling until tomatillos change color from vibrant green to more of a lighter green, about 10 minutes.

While the tomatillos are cooking, in a cast iron skillet, add the olive oil. When the pan is warmed up, add the peppers, garlic cloves and onion slices, and pan fry on medium to medium low heat. Cooking slow and steady, and turning occasionally, soften, and cook through. All should be nicely browned and easily pierced with a fork. In a high-speed blender, add drained tomatillos and the onions, peppers and garlic, plus **1/2** cup cooking liquid to start (sometimes I add chicken broth). Add the salt, lime juice and the cilantro. Blend well. If the sauce is too thick, drizzle in a little more liquid.

Pour out into skillet and bring to a high simmer for about 2-3 minutes. Remove from the heat, and at this point, the master sauce is done! See the following steps for what you choose to make with the sauce, or cool, portion and freeze in 1 and 2 cup portions.

continued ⟶

CHILAQUILES

Having eaten Mexican food my whole life (thanks Mom!), it's hard to believe that I had my first chilaquiles a few years ago when my son Nolan and I were searching out colleges. It was such an indulgence, I had to come home and make some. I already had my sauce, so I put the dish together like it was served in the restaurant. Sometimes, I just like to use the chips for making a batch of nachos.
Serves 3-4

▌INGREDIENTS

8 organic corn tortillas

Drizzle of olive oil

Grey salt

Crock pot taco meat or shredded chicken (recipe not included), about 2-3 cups

2-3 cups master tomatillo sauce

TOPPING SUGGESTIONS
▌INGREDIENTS

Shredded iceberg lettuce

Tomato, chopped

Cotija cheese, crumbled

Avocado, diced and drizzled with lime juice

Sliced black olives

Cumin lime crema or sour cream

Lime wedges

Preheat oven to 450°F. Working with 4 tortillas at a time, rub olive oil on both sides with your fingers. Stack the tortillas and cut in half and then cut each half into thirds. Spread tortillas out on a large baking sheet and sprinkle lightly with the salt. Do the same for the remaining 4 tortillas. Place the baking tray in the oven on the top third rack and bake for 8 minutes. At this point, chips are ready for nacho toppings or read on for how I make the chilaquiles.

Add 2 cups tomatillo sauce to a hot skillet and toss in some corn chips. Add in more sauce if necessary. Stir around and add in the **crock pot taco meat** or shredded chicken and continue to simmer a few minutes stirring all around.

Scoop out a serving onto a plate or shallow bowl and top with shredded lettuce, crumbled cotija cheese and a drizzle of sour cream or **cumin lime crema**. Serve with lime wedges. This is also nice with a side of the **pinto beans**.

ENCHILADAS

Makes 8

▌INGREDIENTS

1 pack of organic corn tortillas

2-3 cups **master tomatillo sauce**

Crock pot taco meat, or shredded chicken (recipe not included)

1 onion, diced

Cotija cheese

Cilantro, chopped

Keep the sauce warm on low until preparing tortillas. In a 6x8 casserole dish sprayed lightly with coconut spray, add a couple spoonfuls of the sauce and spread to lightly cover the bottom of the dish.

Preheat oven to 400°F. Working one at a time, place tortilla on a plate, put a spoonful of sauce (about a table-spoon) on the tortilla, and swirl it around with the back of the spoon to cover the tortilla. Spread meat of choice horizontally across the bottom, just a little lower from the middle of the tortilla. Sprinkle on a little cheese, then roll the tortilla up and place seam side down in the casserole dish. When all are rolled and fit snugly in the dish, spoon and evenly spread the sauce over the top being sure to get the sides too. Top with some cotija cheese and bake for 15 minutes on the middle rack, then broil for 2-3 minutes until golden.

When done, remove from the oven and sprinkle with diced onion and cilantro on the top and serve with **crema** of choice and side of **guacamole**, if desired.

continued ⟶

CUMIN LIME CREMA

Use these two toppings to compliment any Mexican dish.

🚩 **INGREDIENTS**

1/2 cup sour cream

1/2 teaspoon ground cumin

1 tablespoon lime juice

Pinch of salt mix

In a small bowl, mix all ingredients and place in the fridge until serving.

TOMATILLO CREMA

🚩 **INGREDIENTS**

1/2 cup **master tomatillo sauce**

1/4 cup sour cream

Squeeze of lime juice

1 tablespoon cilantro, chopped, optional

In a small bowl, mix all ingredients. Taste for seasoning and place in fridge until serving.

Tomatillo Blossoms

TOSTADAS

This serves as many as you want to make. Here I made 5 from leftover crock pot taco meat I pulled out of the freezer, which always makes for an easy meal.

Serves 2-3

▌ INGREDIENTS

5 corn tortillas

Crock pot taco meat

Pinto beans for a crowd or ***easy weeknight pinto beans***, or any beans of choice

Shredded lettuce and cilantro

Lime juice

Pepper jack cheese slices

Guacamole for the top, with 1 small mango, peeled, diced and mixed in, if desired

Cilantro for garnish, if desired

Lime wedges for serving

Variety of mixed hot peppers, minced for those who like to sprinkle on top

Tomatillo crema

Preheat broiler to HIGH. Pan fry corn tortillas one at a time in a drizzle of grapeseed oil on a comal or any hot skillet, about a minute per side. Using tongs, flip to the other side and move around in the oil. Remove to drain on paper towels. When all are done, place on a large baking sheet covered in parchment.

On each tortilla, spoon a layer of refried pinto beans spreading evenly. Add a layer of the shredded lettuce and sprinkle on the taco meat. Cover with the cheese and place in the oven. Broil for 5-7 minutes until cheese is melted and golden. Serve with guacamole on top, sprinkled cilantro, lime wedge, tomatillo crema and a side bowl of minced hot peppers.

FRESH GARDEN TOMATILLO SALSA

This salsa is so refreshing and delicious with taco chips. Make it as spicy as you want!

▌ INGREDIENTS

12-14 tomatillos cut in half and then half again

Any hot pepper of choice, such as jalapeño or red serrano, seeded and chopped

4 garlic cloves

1/4 of a small sweet onion

1/2 bunch cilantro

1/2 teaspoon salt mix

Lime juice to taste

Add the garlic and jalapeño to a food processor and whiz up. Add all other ingredients and pulse blend until you have a nice chunky consistency, but well mixed. Taste for seasoning and serve with taco chips, or use as a topper for tacos or tostadas.

continued ⟶

PAN ROASTED TOMATILLO SAUCE

*This sauce is based on my tomatillo salsa and makes a nice condiment for any fiesta dish. This is also the sauce I use to make my creamy enchilada sauce by simply adding a **1/2** cup sour cream to 2 cups sauce.*

▌ INGREDIENTS

1 pound tomatillos, skinned, rinsed and cut in half or left whole if smaller sized

1/2 small red onion

1 garlic clove

1 jalapeño, seeded and quartered

Pinch of salt

Juice of 1 lime

1/2 bunch cilantro or 1 cup packed with stalks

1/2 teaspoon salt

In a cast iron skillet lightly sprayed with coconut oil on medium heat, add all the ingredients. Brown nicely and flip over with tongs so as not to burn, about 10-15 minutes. When all are browning well and the pan begins to dry out, add the juice of half the lime. When the onion and pepper are soft, add all to the blender. Add the cilantro, the juice from the other half of the lime and the salt. Blend well.

If using immediately, pour into a non-reactive saucepan and warm gently. Or, this can be made ahead and stored in the fridge for a few days or in the freezer. If you freeze it, do not add the sour cream.

vegetables & SIDES

To me, nothing beats a great vegetable dish, served on its own, or as a side. They are the supporting stars complimenting a fabulous main dish and completing a memorable dinner. Here you will find some mouthwatering sides that accompany any of the main meals in this book, or keep vegetarian by serving several together.

GERMAN POTATO SALAD

German potato salad is one of our favorites, but I wanted to make it without adding sugar, so I figured sweet onion would lend the sweetness that is the signature, along with the vinegar and bacon, to a great German potato salad. I got the idea one day while roasting onions and garlic for **Nolan's onion dip** and **hot sauce**. I think you'll really enjoy this version!

Serves 6-8 or more at a gathering with other side dishes

FOR THE ROASTED ONIONS, GARLIC AND HOT PEPPER

▌ INGREDIENTS

1/2 of a roasted medium sweet onion, such as Vidalia or Walla Walla, plus 1 tablespoon liquid from roasting the onions, garlic and hot pepper, see *roasting onions* with *Nolan's onion dip*, see **note** on next page

FOR THE POTATOES AND BACON

▌ INGREDIENTS

1 5-pound bag Yukon gold potatoes, peeled and cut in half if all a similar size

1 pack Niman Ranch maple bacon, cut in crosswise slices (lardons), browned in pan, drained, or prepare **baked bacon** and then crumble it with your hands

Add potatoes to a large pot of water and bring to a boil. Add some salt to the pot once the water is boiling. Cook potatoes until easily pierced with a knife, but don't overcook so they are falling apart. Drain in a colander and place some paper towels over the top to absorb moisture as they cool. Thanks, Ina Garten for this tip! When the potatoes are cool enough to handle, but still quite warm, cut into small chunks and add to a large bowl.

Borage

FOR THE DRESSING

▌INGREDIENTS

1/2 cup mayonnaise

1/2 of a roasted medium sweet onion

4 extra-large roasted garlic cloves

1 tablespoon liquid from roasting the onions, garlic and hot pepper

2 tablespoons apple cider vinegar

1 1/2 tablespoons Dijon mustard

1 roasted Bangalore pepper or any pepper you like, optional

1 teaspoon salt

Freshly ground black pepper

1/4 cup chives, chopped, reserving half to sprinkle on top

1/4 cup parsley, chopped, reserving half to sprinkle on top

Fresh borage or chive flowers

Add the first 9 ingredients for the dressing into a food processor and blend well. Turn into a medium bowl and add half of the chives and half of the parsley, saving the rest to sprinkle on top.

To the bowl of warm potatoes, add half of the dressing to start. Gently fold in the dressing, half of the bacon, and half of the chives and parsley, continuing to add more to reach your desired amount. Use a spatula to transfer to a serving bowl or platter. Sprinkle with the remaining, chives, parsley, and bacon and decorate with borage or chive flowers.

Note: If you aren't planning on making the onion dip in the next few days, roast only one onion with the garlic and hot pepper, if desired. You could even just roast 4 cloves of garlic in the skin instead of the whole head, but I like having it around. Adding the dressing to the warm potatoes helps the flavors soak in.

ZUCCHINI FRIES

I promise if you serve these instead of regular fries you won't get any complaints!

Serves 4

▌ INGREDIENTS

8 4-inch zucchini, ends trimmed
   and cut into 4 fries, or 1
   extra-large zucchini seeded
   and cut into 24 fries

Salt mix

3 large eggs, blended

3 cups *gluten-free Italian
   seasoned breadcrumbs*, or
   any breadcrumbs

1 cup Parmigiano-Reggiano
   cheese, finely grated

On a clean kitchen towel or paper towels, spread out the fries and sprinkle with a little salt. Let sit 30 minutes to extract water and then pat dry. In a medium bowl, add the breadcrumbs and mix in the finely grated parmesan cheese. In another bowl, beat the eggs.

Preheat oven to 450°F. On a large baking sheet, rub with a drizzle of extra virgin olive oil. With one hand, dip each zucchini fry in the egg and transfer to the breadcrumbs. With your other hand, coat the zucchini in the bread-crumbs (keeping one hand for wet and one for dry). Place each one on the baking sheet leaving space between each one. When all are done, lightly spray with coconut oil. Place on the upper rack and bake for 15 minutes. Check and let go another 5-7 minutes more.

Transfer to a platter and serve with *special sauce* if desired.

BAKED BROCCOLI CHIPS

I love using any hearty green to make "chips" and I made several batches with a few plants in the garden thinking they were collard greens, then one day I saw the broccoli florets growing. I had been making broccoli chips all along! Substitute any of your favorite greens for these.

⚑ INGREDIENTS

Large bowlful of greens washed and dried, stalks removed and ripped into big chips

1/2-1 tablespoon drizzle of extra virgin olive oil or coconut oil

Salt mix

Freshly ground black pepper

OPTIONAL ADD-ONS

Grated Parmigiano-Reggiano or Pecorino Romano cheese

Nutritional yeast

Herbs

Smoked salt

Preheat oven to 325°F.

Place dried greens in a large bowl. Drizzle on the oil and with your hands, massage the oil onto each leaf. On prepared baking sheet lined with parchment, spread the leaves in one layer. Sprinkle with salt and black pepper, if desired. Bake on the middle rack of the oven for 8 minutes. Rotate pan and cook another 5-8 minutes keeping a close eye. Remove from the oven and slide the parchment off onto the counter. The chips will cool and get crunchy. Eat as a snack or as a side with any meal.

CURLICUE YUKONS

These potatoes are irresistible and remind me of potato sticks. Don't worry if some get crisper than others, I guarantee someone will be grabbing for them.

Serves 4

▌ INGREDIENTS

8 medium Yukon gold potatoes with skin, cleaned and dried

1/4 cup extra virgin olive oil

ROSEMARY SPRINKLE

1 tablespoon rosemary, finely minced

1 teaspoon salt mix

Freshly ground black pepper

1 tablespoon chopped parsley for garnish

Preheat oven to 425°F.

Using a spiralizer with the large hole attachment, spiralize the potatoes and place on top of a paper towel lined large bowl. Layer paper towels between potatoes as you spiralize them, and when all are done, gently pat them dry. Mix rosemary with the salt and pepper. Add the olive oil and rosemary sprinkle to the potatoes, and with both hands, toss gently and massage to coat them well. Spread potatoes evenly on a lightly sprayed large baking sheet and roast about 35 minutes. When golden, take out of the oven and sprinkle with extra salt and herbs.

Serve immediately.

TWICE BAKED ITALIAN STYLE RED POTATOES WITH BASIL PESTO

This recipe came about like 95 percent of my recipes - from what I'm craving and from the ingredients I have on hand. This comes together quickly, especially if the pesto is made the day before or you have some leftover. Try substituting any of the pestos in this book.

Serves 7 (or 4-5 hungry kids)

▌INGREDIENTS

7 medium red potatoes (could do 6 or 8 with 1/2-3/4 cup pesto)

3/4 cup basil pesto

5-6 slices prosciutto di Parma

Provolone cheese slices

1/4 cup Parmigiano-Reggiano cheese, grated

Chives, chopped for garnish

Preheat oven to 400°F. Scrub the potatoes, pierce each with a knife, and bake directly on the rack (I like my toaster oven for this), about 1 hour and 10 minutes (test with a knife). Let cool so as to be able to handle them. Slice off about a **1/4** of the top of each potato and scoop out most of the potato into a medium bowl, leaving some on the skin so it holds its shape. Mash in the pesto just until mixed, taste for seasoning and mound back into the skins, placing all on a lightly sprayed baking sheet. If adding some of the prosciutto crisps, wait until they are done before filling the potato skins.

Meanwhile bake the prosciutto crisps. Lay 5-6 slices prosciutto on parchment paper and bake about 8 minutes. You can add these into the same oven with the potatoes during the last 8 minutes of cooking time. Cool and crumble. Mix some into the potatoes if you wish before mounding back into skins, but save enough to sprinkle on each potato.

Top each potato with **1/4** slice provolone cheese and sprinkling of Parmigiano. Bake about 20-25 minutes being sure to keep an eye. When cheese is melted and golden, remove from the oven and transfer carefully to a serving platter. Top with crumbled prosciutto crisps and chopped chives and serve.

ZUCCHINI CAKE FRITTERS TWO WAYS

We just love fritters, burgers, cakes, latkes....whatever you want to call them, they are excellent! And in summer when you are bombarded with zucchini and see some beauties at the farmer's market, this is the best way to use them up. First way makes a thicker cake I use as burger buns, but you could eat it just like a burger! Second way makes a great side dish to just about anything.

WAY #1 – MORE BUN-LIKE WITH KALE

■ INGREDIENTS

Extra virgin olive oil for pan frying

2 medium zucchinis, see **note**

8 ounces chopped frozen kale, thawed and squeezed of liquid

2 eggs, blended

3/4 cup breadcrumbs, any kind, or see any of the **gluten-free breadcrumbs**

1/2 cup scallions, diced fine, about 3

1/4 cup basil, chopped

1 large garlic clove, minced

1/2 teaspoon baking powder

Zest of 1 lemon

1/2 teaspoon salt mix, or to taste

Freshly ground black pepper

Cut the ends off the zucchini and then slice lengthwise in half. If there are any large seeds, scrape them out with a spoon. Shred the zucchini on the large holes of the box grater or in a food processor with the shredder blade. Place all the zucchini in a sieve set over a bowl and sprinkle with salt. This will release some liquid. Toss the zucchini and press down with the back of a spoon every 10 minutes or so while preparing the rest of the ingredients. In another large bowl, add all the other ingredients except the breadcrumbs and olive oil. Mix well, and after about 30 minutes, squeeze dry the zucchini and add to the bowl along with the breadcrumbs, mixing well.

On medium heat, add a drizzle of olive oil to a non-stick skillet. Using a **1/3** cup measure, scoop to form patties, then pat into shape with your hands. Pan fry until golden on one side, about 8-10 minutes, then flip and cook the other side. Drain on paper towels and sprinkle with a pinch of salt. As you keep forming the patties, liquid will accumulate in the bowl. Don't worry about this, just squeeze out liquid and form the cake. Eat alongside your meal or use as buns for the turkey burgers.

Note: I have no idea where I heard this tip, but I have been doing it for as long as I can remember. To remove any bitterness from a large zucchini, after cutting the ends off, rub each cut piece on the opposite end in a circular motion and you will see white stuff appear. Rub this off with a paper towel and do the same to the other side.

Note: See picture of these fritters with the **turkey burgers for the 4th.**

WAY #2 – MORE LATKE-LIKE

Use your biggest zucchini for these as they are just perfect for making these more latke-like fritters.
Preheat oven to 300°F *if you want to keep the cakes warm for serving.*

▌ INGREDIENTS

Extra virgin olive oil for sautéing

1-2 tablespoons Kerrygold butter

1 huge zucchini

6 scallions, thinly sliced

2 large garlic cloves, minced

2 eggs, blended

1/2 cup basil, chopped

1 teaspoon grey salt

Lots of freshly ground black pepper

Cut the ends off the zucchini and then slice lengthwise in half. If there are any large seeds, scrape them out with a spoon. Shred the zucchini on the large holes of the box grater or in a food processor with the shredder blade. Place all the zucchini in a sieve set over a bowl and sprinkle with salt. This will release some liquid. Toss the zucchini and press down with the back of a spoon every 10 minutes or so while preparing the rest of the ingredients.

In another large bowl, add all the other ingredients, except the olive oil and butter, and after about 30 minutes squeeze dry the zucchini and add to the bowl. Mix well.

On medium heat add a drizzle of olive oil and a half tablespoon of butter in a non-stick skillet. Using a **1/3** cup measure, scoop to form patties, then pat into shape with your hands. Pan fry until golden on one side, about 8-10 minutes, then flip and cook the other side, lightly salting the flipped side. As you keep forming the patties, liquid will accumulate in the bowl. Don't worry about this, just squeeze out liquid and form the latke. When nice and golden on second side, remove and place on a parchment paper lined baking sheet and keep warm in the oven until all are done. Eat alongside your meal or top a salad with a few for a nice light lunch.

SAUTÉED LAMBS QUARTERS

Lambs quarters grow out of control in the garden and keeping up with them is harder said than done. They are so flavorful sautéed here the way we usually do spinach, or added fresh to a smoothie or juice. By end of summer when we can't keep up, they are towering higher than the fence!

Serves 2

▌INGREDIENTS

1 big bunch garden lambs quarters, about 12, thicker stalks removed, but leaving small tender stalks, washed and spun dry, see *note,* or spinach

1 garlic clove, minced

1 tablespoon Kerrygold butter

1 tablespoon extra-virgin olive oil

Pinch of salt mix

Freshly ground black pepper

1/4 cup chicken broth or water, optional

Lemon wedges if desired

Melt the butter and heat up with the olive oil in large sauté pan. Add the minced garlic and stir around a minute, then add in the lambs quarters. Season with a pinch of salt and freshly ground black pepper. Let cook and continue to stir until wilted and garlic is slightly golden. If you need to, add the broth or water and simmer a few minutes.

Note: Lambs quarters are amazing and can grow 8-10 feet or more, producing upwards of 75,000 seeds per plant! They are also full of Vitamins, such as A, B, and C. They contain iron, calcium, phosphorus and potassium, making them great for the bones. High in protein, and as with all dark leafy greens, they are anti-inflammatory.

ROASTED ROSEMARY GARLIC BUTTERCREAM POTATOES

Way back in good ole 1995, I was given a cookbook from my mother and father-in-law simply called Roasting, by Barbara Kafka, and she forever changed the way I cook potatoes. If I had to pick one thing I could live on, it would most likely be these potatoes.

Serves 3-4

INGREDIENTS

2 -3 pounds garden buttercream or fingerling potatoes, washed, un-peeled and cut into half to 1 inch chunks, see *note*

1/3-1/2 cup olive oil

3 sprigs rosemary, each about 6 inches long

3 garlic cloves, minced, or in a pinch, 1/2 teaspoon garlic powder (But the garlic crunchies after roasting is what everyone wants!)

3/4 teaspoon salt mix

Freshly ground black pepper

Preheat oven to 450°F. Lightly spray a 9x13 glass casserole dish, or larger (they need to be in a single layer). Place potatoes in a large bowl and blot dry with paper towels. Strip the leaves from the rosemary stalks and mince. Place in a small bowl. Add the minced garlic, or garlic powder, salt and pepper. Pour in the olive oil and mix. Pour onto the potatoes and mix well. Turn the potatoes into the baking dish and scrape the remaining oil with a spatula, again, making sure they are in a single layer.

Roast for 20 minutes, then toss the potatoes around with a spatula. Roast another 20 minutes. Toss the potatoes again then roast a final 20 minutes. Potatoes should be golden brown. In prepared serving dish, place down a paper towel and with a spatula scoop out the potatoes while with one hand you are draining the oil to one end of the baking dish. Sprinkle potatoes with salt and remove the paper towel and serve.

Note: Use any of your favorite potatoes for this dish – they are all fantastic. If I'm using a larger potato or any potatoes that have spots, I peel them and continue with the recipe. Sometimes, it's nice to have them peeled, but when the skin is blemish free, I keep it on for the extra nutrients.

SUMMER GRILLED VEGETABLES

I love grilling a variety of vegetables and peppers in the summer. The colorful combinations are literally endless and the local markets have even more variety – use what you have and toss it all on the grill.

🚩 INGREDIENTS

4 large portobello mushrooms, stems removed and gills scraped out with a spoon

2 large Vidalia onions cut into nice 3/4 inch thick slices

4 medium zucchini squash sliced 1/4 inch lengthwise

6-8 garden hot peppers, optional, such as Anaheim, spicy banana, or Hungarian

MARINADE FOR MUSHROOMS & PEPPERS

1/3 cup extra virgin olive oil

2 tablespoons balsamic vinegar

2 garlic cloves, minced

1/4 mixed herbs rosemary, basil, chives, chopped fine

Salt and pepper

MARINADE FOR SQUASH & PEPPERS

1/4 cup extra virgin olive oil

2 tablespoons lemon juice

Zest of 1 lemon

1/4 cup mixed herbs thyme, basil, chives

Salt and pepper

Mix the ingredients for the marinades in small bowls separately, or just drizzle and add directly to the platter of prepared vegetables, which is what I usually do. Otherwise, place the veggies on 2 platters and pour each marinade over. Rub and coat the vegetables on all sides with your hands. If grilling peppers, be sure and pierce each one with a sharp knife so they don't explode on the grill – yes it has happened before!

Grill on medium to medium low turning occasionally until nicely cooked and peppers retain some crispness. After grilling, return the vegetables to their specific platters with the marinade. Serve with any grilled meat or for a vegetarian meal, serve with a side of rice or potatoes.

GRILLED VEGETABLE AND PEPPER PLATTERS

Serving dishes all on one platter, especially for outdoor eating, makes it so easy because then you don't have too many dishes to carry out, or to cleanup. And I don't know what it is about thyme and basil - they just make a great match with grilled vegetables.

Serves 3-4

🏷 INGREDIENTS

Extra virgin olive oil to drizzle

1 zucchini, sliced lengthwise into 1/4 inch strips

4 hot cherry red peppers, pierce each at the stem end with a knife

6 shitake mushroom caps, stalks removed

1 orange bell pepper, seeded and quartered, or any color bell pepper

Bunch of thyme leaves, chopped about 1/4 cup, or basil

Lemon juice

Salt mix

Freshly ground black pepper

Wash, dry, and prepare the vegetables and peppers. Place them all on a large platter. Drizzle with the oil and squeeze on some lemon juice. Sprinkle on the chopped thyme or basil. Season with salt and freshly ground black pepper.

Rub the marinade all over so all the vegetables are coated. Grill on medium to medium low heat, turning until nicely cooked and peppers still retain some crispness. Remove vegetables as they are done to the original platter with the marinade. Some cook up faster than others. Feel free to slice up a large garden tomato and fan out on the end of the platter. Sprinkle on more herbs and serve. Make as many varied platters as you need to feed a crowd.

TWO VARIATIONS USING THE SAME METHOD

▌ INGREDIENTS

1 large red onion, sliced into 1/4 inch thick slices

1 red bell pepper, seeded and quartered

1 orange bell pepper, seeded and quartered

1 medium zucchini, ends trimmed, sliced lengthwise into 1/4 inch thick strips

▌ INGREDIENTS

1 large sweet onion, sliced into 1/4-1/2 inch thick sliced

2 medium Yukon gold potatoes

4 shitake mushrooms, stalks removed

6 garden variety of hot peppers, cut lengthwise, seeds removed

This variation uses basil instead of thyme and a splash of Italian vinegar on the potatoes, or use any vinegar, such as balsamic.

SPICY PURPLE CABBAGE COLESLAW

This is a nice change from the usual picnic coleslaw and it feeds a crowd. If you don't want it spicy, just leave out the chili pepper and add the honey. It makes a colorful addition to any table!

Serves 10-12

▌INGREDIENTS

6 cups purple cabbage, thinly sliced, about half of a medium cabbage

1 red bell pepper, thinly sliced, pat moisture off with a paper towel, or yellow bell

3 scallions, sliced

Handful of cilantro, chopped

Sesame seeds, optional for garnish

FOR THE SAUCE

1/4 cup tahini, see *my cupboard*

1 1/2 tablespoons toasted sesame oil

1 1/2 tablespoons raw local clover honey, optional

1 large garlic clove, minced

2 tablespoons lime juice

2 tablespoons lemon juice

1 tablespoon gluten-free soy sauce, low sodium

1/4 teaspoon red devils tongue dried chili powder, or any dried chili pepper powder

In a large bowl, add the cabbage, bell pepper and scallions and some of the chopped cilantro, reserving some to sprinkle on top. Mix together all the ingredients for the sauce and keep in the fridge until ready to toss with the slaw. Sauce may also be made ahead. Some tahini is thicker than others, so if it is too thick, add a dash water or more lemon or lime juice.

Coleslaw may be tossed together about an hour before serving, but not much longer or the cabbage becomes too watery. When ready to serve, place in a pretty serving bowl or on a shallow platter and sprinkle on a little more cilantro and sesame seeds, if desired.

ZUCCHINI PARMIGIANA

What a fun take on traditional parmigiana! Instead of tomato sauce, this recipe incorporates fresh garden tomatoes and showcases another great way to utilize your huge garden or market zucchini. Serves 4-6

🔖 INGREDIENTS

Eight 1/2-inch thick slices, from a large zucchini, cut crosswise into circles

2 cups tomatoes of choice, finely seeded and diced

6 fresh basil leaves, sliced chiffonade into long thin strips

1 cup Italian seasoned breadcrumbs, or see *gluten-free Italian seasoned breadcrumbs*

1 cup Parmigiano-Reggiano cheese, finely grated

Freshly ground black pepper

Your best olive oil for drizzling

Preheat oven to 350°F. Begin by trimming the ends of the zucchini, cut into half inch thick rounds. With a small spoon, scoop out the center of each one removing the seeds. Lay on paper towels and sprinkle with a little salt to extract some liquid. Meanwhile, in a medium bowl, add the diced tomatoes, basil, 2 tablespoons of the breadcrumbs, 1 tablespoon of the cheese, and freshly ground black pepper.

Line a baking sheet with parchment paper. Place a hollow top from a ball jar (one about the same size as your zucchini rounds) upside down on the parchment and spread **11/2** tablespoons of parmesan to create 8 circles of cheese. Pat the zucchini dry and place the zucchini rounds on top of the cheese. Fill the centers with the tomato mixture. Top with seasoned breadcrumbs and a sprinkling of cheese. Lightly drizzle a little extra virgin olive oil over each one.

Bake for 20 to 25 minutes until golden brown, being sure to let cool for 5 minutes before gently removing from the parchment with a spatula.

BUTTERNUT SQUASH LATKES

You will not believe how incredibly delectable these are! They make a great side dish to any meal. Makes about 8 latkes with a small squash and 10 with a medium.

INGREDIENTS

1 small to medium butternut squash peeled, seeded, and shredded, about 4 cups

1/2 medium onion, shredded

1 egg, blended

1 teaspoon fresh sage, minced

1 teaspoon fresh rosemary, minced

1 teaspoon salt mix

Freshly ground black pepper

Butter and extra virgin olive oil for pan frying

In a medium bowl, add all ingredients, except the butter and olive oil, and mix well. In a non-stick or cast iron skillet, drop by spoonfuls and pat down gently with the back of the spoon. Cook on medium heat until golden, about 15 minutes a side. If you try and flip too soon, they start to fall apart, so let cook until golden, and they will easily flip when ready. Flip and cook the other side. If heat gets too high, turn down a notch so they don't burn.

When all are done, arrange on a serving platter. We like to serve with **sautéed lambs quarters** or any sautéed greens.

Note: Try substituting 1 teaspoon minced fresh thyme and 1 teaspoon dried Herbes de Provence for the sage and rosemary.

THICK-CUT POTATO CHIPS

These are so tasty with a side of guacamole to dip into, or just spread it on the top for an amazing indulgence. They even make a great hors d'oeuvre or a simple vegetarian dinner by adding toppings!

Serves 2-4

▌INGREDIENTS

2 large russet potatoes, washed and peeled

2 tablespoons olive oil

Herbes de Provence, or any dried herb of choice

Salt mix

Freshly ground black pepper

Preheat oven to 400°F. With coconut oil cooking spray, give a quick spray to a baking sheet just to prevent sticking. Slice potatoes into **1/4** thick slices lengthwise or into rounds. Pat dry and place in large bowl. Drizzle on the olive oil, pinch or two of any herb of choice, salt and pepper. Toss, making sure potatoes are coated on both sides. Place on the baking sheet in a single layer.

Bake for 20 minutes, then take out of the oven and flip each one. I like using two forks for this, or my mini tongs. Place back in the oven for another 20 minutes. Depending on your oven, these may take a little less time, or a little more, just check often. You want them to be nice and golden brown. If some are done before others, remove them to the serving dish and place the others back in the oven.

When done, transfer to a serving dish with a side of **guacamole**, if desired, or they are equally scrumptious on their own. To make it a dinner, put anything you love on top, such as **sautéed lambs quarters** or kale, chopped lettuce, olives or just a sprinkle of herbs or hot peppers. SO GOOD!

ITALIAN ZUCCHINI TOMATO BAKE

Here is another great way to use any overgrown squash and too many ripe tomatoes, or an over-loaded CSA basket. This also makes a perfect dish to bring along to any cookout.

Serves 6-8

▌INGREDIENTS

1 overgrown zucchini or yellow crookneck squash

2-3 medium to large tomatoes, seeded and cut into wedges

large handful sliced basil, about 1/2 cup

2 shallots, slivered

4 garlic cloves, minced

1 cup fresh Italian seasoned breadcrumbs, or *gluten-free Italian seasoned breadcrumbs*, or *gluten-free Italian style panko breadcrumbs*

3/4 cup finely grated, lightly packed Parmigiano-Reggiano cheese

Olive oil for drizzling

Grey salt

Freshly ground black pepper

Preheat oven to 350°F. In a large casserole dish, lightly spray with oil. Starting with the zucchini, slice lengthwise and with a spoon, scrape out the seeds. Then cut cross-wise into half-moons, about a half inch thick. Sprinkle the slices around the casserole dish. Next, cut the tomatoes in half and take out the seeds with a small knife, then cut into wedges and place those in and around the zucchini. Do the same with the shallots and garlic, sprinkling evenly over the zucchini and tomatoes. Sprinkle on the basil. Lightly salt and pepper.

Mix the Parmigiano and the breadcrumbs together and sprinkle over the casserole and drizzle olive oil over the top. Cover lightly with foil, tenting slightly so it doesn't stick to the breadcrumb cheese topping and bake 25 minutes. Take the cover off and bake another 20 minutes or until the top is nice and golden.

JASMINE RICE

*This is my favorite rice for making **Chinese style vegetable fried rice**. Making fluffy rice is a surprising challenge - I have learned the hard way that not soaking your rice beforehand leaves you with glue. Believe me when I say soak, rinse, soak, rinse, and repeat until the water is clear, or almost clear, but not cloudy. If I know I'm serving rice, I start this process at least one to two hours before cooking, if not longer. Start while preparing other parts of your meal.*

Serves 6

▍INGREDIENTS

2 cups jasmine rice

2 cups filtered water

In a medium saucepan, add the rice and water. Bring to the boil and stir with a slotted spoon about a minute until the water is level or just below the rice. Turn heat to low, cover and cook 5-7 minutes. I check after 5 minutes because soaking and rinsing makes the cook time shorter, and all rice is different. When done, move off the hot burner, fluff with a fork, and keep the cover tilted for steam to escape. Serve alongside any meal or chill and save for fried rice.

HERBY SPRING RISOTTO WITH LETTUCE

*I usually make some variety of risotto a couple times a year just to make the **crispy baked arancini di riso** (rice balls). We absolutely love them.*

Serves 6 as part of a meal

INGREDIENTS

1 1/2 tablespoon Kerrygold butter

1/2 cup onion, finely diced

1/2 cup inner celery with leaves, finely diced

1/2 cup leeks, finely diced

1/3 cup any white wine, such as Clos du Bois, or extra dry vermouth, or substitute with a 1/4 cup lemon juice

1 cup carnaroli rice, see **my cupboard**

4 cups chicken broth, warmed

1 1/2 cups inner romaine lettuce leaves or butter lettuce, thinly sliced

3/4 cup grated Parmigiano-Reggiano cheese, plus a little more for the top

1/4 cup chopped mint

1/4 cup chopped chives, reserving some to sprinkle on top

In a medium saucepan, melt the butter and add the onion, celery and leeks. Cook until translucent, but not turning color. Add the rice and stir well to coat in the butter. Deglaze with the wine, or lemon juice, and let cook until all absorbed, just a few minutes. Add a cup of broth at a time, adding another cup when most absorbed. Stir every now and again.

You may not need all 4 cups broth – sometimes 3 1/2 cups is perfect, just taste the rice to make sure it is creamy but still a touch al dente (firm to the bite).

When just done, stir in the cheese, lettuce, mint, and chives. Serve with a sprinkling of chives and cheese on top. This risotto goes great with anything grilled. And of course, if you want to make just for the arancini, make a day ahead so the rice will be cold.

CRUNCHY CUCUMBERS

Remember those sweet and vinegary cukes from summer that go just right with about any meal? These are simple to make and you can adjust the recipe to make them as sweet or vinegary as you remember.

▌ INGREDIENTS

2 long garden cucumbers, Armenian or Japanese, suyo long, or English

1 1/2-2 teaspoons salt mix

1 small sweet onion or red onion, sliced into half-moons, optional

1/4 cup distilled white vinegar or rice wine vinegar

1/4 cup Braggs apple cider vinegar (do not use clear vinegar)

1/4-1/2 cup water depending on how vinegary you like it

1 1/2 tablespoons or more sugar, or more to taste

1/2 teaspoon Dijon mustard, optional

Few sprigs dill, either chopped or left whole, or few sprigs tarragon is also nice

Pinch freshly ground black pepper

Take each cucumber (peel completely if coated in wax) and make 4-5 lengthwise strips with a vegetable peeler to leave some of the skin on or peel completely if you wish. I like to take each long cucumber and cut it in half for slicing very thin on a mandolin or the slicer on the side of a box grater or cutting by hand with a sharp knife. Once each half is sliced, I layer the pieces in a non-reactive colander set over a bowl and sprinkle with a **1/2** teaspoon salt. By the time all the cucumbers are sliced and placed into the colander, you will have used most or all of the salt. Let the cucumbers sit to extract the water. This part takes a couple of hours and feel free to put a weighted plate on top of them if you want.

After a couple of hours, give the cucumbers a quick rinse under running water and then lay them on paper towels or a clean kitchen towel and pat them dry. Place in a non-reactive bowl. Cut the onion in half and thinly slice into half-moons separating the slices. Add to the cucumbers and toss together.

In a small bowl, add the vinegars, water, and stir in the sugar, Dijon if using, and the dill. This step may be done while the cucumbers sit. When sugar is dissolved, pour over the rinsed and patted dry cucumbers. Using tongs transfer to a mason jar or glass container of choice and pour over the liquid. Give the liquid a taste to see if you want to add a pinch more sugar. Try and let sit overnight in the fridge. Keeps for weeks and taste better the longer they sit. Serve alongside any meal, but also great with potato salad or top a burger or dog for a refreshing crunchy bite.

stuffed STUFF

We love stuffed stuff as much as we love our dips and spreads, and often the two join each other.

CRISPY BAKED ARANCINI DI RISO
(ITALIAN RICE BALLS STUFFED WITH MOZZARELLA CHEESE OR WITH BEEF AND MOZZARELLA CHEESE)

*When the kids were little they used to love helping make these crispy creamy rice balls. I also used to hide spinach in there! The smaller ones make a great appetizer at a cocktail party and the larger ones make the perfect side dish. You can even make a dinner out of them by stuffing with the **beef and mozzarella filling**, or keep it simple and just add the cheese. Either way, everyone is always psyched when they see these come to the table.*

FOR THE MOZZARELLA FILLING
Makes about 20 small balls.

▌ **INGREDIENTS**

3 cups or so leftover **herby spring risotto**, or any risotto

Fresh mozzarella cheese cut into 1/2 inch, or smaller cubes

2 eggs, blended in a small bowl

2-3 cups **gluten-free Italian seasoned breadcrumbs** or **gluten-free Italian style panko**, or any breadcrumbs

Chopped dill for sprinkling on tops

I like to use my 1 inch cookie dough press to make small balls. Wet the press or small spoon, and also your hands. Form all the rice balls and place on a parchment paper lined baking sheet. With wet hands, use your thumb to press a divot in the center of each ball. Add the cheese cube and form the rice over the cheese making sure it is all sealed. Place tray in the fridge until ready to dip and bake.

Preheat oven to 400°F. On prepared baking sheet, spray small circles where you will place each ball. When ready to bake, place the breadcrumbs in a medium bowl. Whichever hand you use, keep one for dry ingredients and one for wet ingredients. Take a ball and roll in the egg and then dip into the crumbs coating well.

Place each one on the baking sheet, then spray the tops and sides lightly when all are done. Place in the oven and bake until nice and golden brown about 20 minutes. Transfer to a serving platter and sprinkle with chopped dill.

FOR THE BEEF AND MOZZARELLA FILLING

*This makes so much more filling than you will need for the leftover **risotto**, but is excellent for adding to a meat sauce. Sometimes I freeze it so I have some ready if I want to make more rice balls, or you could also cut the recipe in half.*

Makes 6 larger balls

▌ INGREDIENTS

3/4-1 pound ground beef

1/2 medium to large onion about 1 cup, finely diced

2 large garlic cloves, minced

1 large celery stalk small dice about 1/2 cup

1 teaspoon dried oregano

1 heaping tablespoon chopped fresh basil, added when filling has cooled

Pinch salt mix

Freshly ground black pepper

3 cups or so leftover risotto

1 container of the tiny balls of fresh mozzarella cheese, or the bigger ones cut into 1/2 inch cubes

2 eggs, blended in a small bowl

2-3 cups *gluten-free Italian seasoned breadcrumbs*, or *gluten-free Italian style panko,* or any breadcrumbs

Rao's arrabiata, marinara, or vodka sauce for dipping, your own homemade if you have it, or your favorite tomato sauce, optional

In a large sauté pan, add a drizzle of olive oil and add the onion, garlic and celery. Season with a pinch of salt and freshly ground black pepper and sauté until soft. Add the beef and cook, breaking up the meat with the back of a spoon. When all meat is all cooked, I pull out my potato masher to get the meat mixture uniform and if there is a lot of fat, I would drain it here. When beef has cooled, add the basil and taste for seasoning.

Preheat oven to 400°F – convection if available. On prepared baking sheet, spray larger circles where you will place each ball. When ready to bake, place the breadcrumbs in a medium bowl. For this filling, I use a **1/4** cup measure for the rice ball, plus an **1/8** of a cup measure for the amount topping the ball once filled. With wet hands form the rice into balls and then with the **1/4** cup size balls, use your thumb to press a divot in the center. Add a small spoonful of the meat mixture, about 2 teaspoons, and then top with the cheese cube. Take the **1/8** cup rice balls and press to the top, making sure all the filling is sealed inside.

Whichever hand you use, keep one for dry ingredients and one for wet ingredients. Take a ball and roll in the egg, and then dip into the breadcrumbs coating well. Place each one on the baking sheet, then spray the tops and sides lightly when all are done. Place in the oven on the middle rack for about 18 minutes, then broil for 2-3 minutes to get nice and golden. Serve with any tomato sauce, if desired.

STUFFED GARDEN BELL PEPPERS

Use 5-6 of any combination of peppers. Everyone loves these, but my daughter Cristina, loves these so much, when she lived at home, she said I should make them once a week! They also freeze well for a quick lunch box meal.

Serves 5 or 4 with lunchbox leftovers

🚩 INGREDIENTS

1-2 large yellow bell pepper

1 green bell pepper

3 red bell peppers or pimiento peppers

1 pound ground beef 93% lean, or 1 pound ground turkey

1 15-ounce can crushed tomatoes with juice, or diced garden tomatoes

1 medium onion, diced

3 large garlic cloves, minced

1 1/2 cups cooked *jasmine rice*

1/4 cup fresh thyme, chopped

1 teaspoon dried oregano

1 teaspoon salt mix

Lots of freshly ground black pepper

1/3 cup extra dry vermouth

1/2 cup water

4 tablespoons tomato paste

Sliced provolone cheese, or grated Dubliner cheese and Parmigiano-Reggiano, mixed to sprinkle on top

Split peppers in half lengthwise and remove the seeds. Sometimes I remove the stem, other times I like it for presentation. Bring a large pot of water to the boil and sprinkle in a teaspoon or so of salt. Place the peppers carefully in the water so they don't splash hot water on your arm. Immediately turn off the heat and let the peppers sit in the pot for 5 minutes. On a paper towel lined baking sheet, use tongs to remove the peppers, and place cut side down to drain while you make the filling. This step may be done ahead in the day and peppers kept in the fridge.

In a large skillet, sauté the onion, beef and garlic until beef is cooked through, breaking up with a spoon as it cooks. Add the thyme, oregano, salt and pepper, and sauté a minute more. Add the cooked rice and tomatoes and cook about 5 minutes until the rice warms through. Taste for seasoning and set aside and make the sauce. This step may also be made ahead.

FOR STUFFING AND COOKING THE PEPPERS

Preheat oven to 350°F. In a small bowl, mix the vermouth, water, and tomato paste and set aside. Lightly spray a 9x13 casserole dish, or any casserole dish you have that fits your peppers. Take the peppers and with a spoon, fill the peppers, mounding with the beef and rice mixture, and arrange them in your baking dish as you fill them. (You may have extra stuffing.)

Spoon a little of the sauce over each pepper and pour the rest around the peppers. Bake for 30 minutes. Then drape the provolone cheese, or cheese of choice over each pepper and continue to bake for 10 more minutes, or until the cheese is melted. Sprinkle with fresh parsley or dill and serve.

SAUSAGE AND CHEESE STUFFED ANAHEIM PEPPERS

Growing up, my parents friend made hors d'oeuvres of sausage cheese toasts on pumpernickel bread, and this filling reminds me of those so much, especially with the herb combination below. These make a nice meal with a side salad, or here with sliced garden tomatoes.

Serves 2-3

▌ INGREDIENTS

6 large Anaheim peppers, prepared for stuffing, see **note**

1 pound sweet Italian sausage, removed from casings

1 tablespoon of extra virgin olive oil

1 medium sweet onion, diced

Pinch salt mix

Freshly ground black pepper

3 garlic cloves, minced

1/8-1/4 cup fresh tarragon and lavender, minced

1/4 cup extra dry vermouth

8 ounces Monterey Jack cheese or Blarney Castle Gouda style cheese, grated

1/2 cup Parmigiano-Reggiano cheese, grated

Prepare peppers first, then in a large frying pan on medium heat, sauté and break up the sausage with a potato masher. Stir, cooking until pink is gone, and place on a plate with paper towels to drain, about 15 minutes. Wipe the pan clean, return to the heat, and add the olive oil, onion, salt, and freshly ground black pepper to taste. Sauté until soft, then add the sausage back to the pan. Add the garlic, tarragon, and lavender to the mixture and cook until the sausage becomes lightly browned. Deglaze the pan with the vermouth, stirring until almost all liquid is absorbed. Taste for seasoning and remove from the heat.

Preheat oven to 350°F. Line a baking sheet with parchment paper. Mix the Monterey Jack cheese, or the Gouda with the Parmigiano-Reggiano cheese, and set aside. Gently open the peppers and using a small spoon, tightly pack in the sausage mixture. Cover the tops with the cheese mixture and place in the oven and bake for 20 minutes. Finally, broil the peppers for 2 minutes, watching closely for a golden brown color. Serve with sliced tomatoes, if desired.

Note: For preparing hot peppers for stuffing, start by slicing a capital T shape into the peppers, top of the T being at the top of the pepper, close to the stem. Then cut lengthwise down the middle. Slightly open the peppers, and scrape out the seeds. I like to dry my seeds to save and you can find information on that in the **miscellaneous** section of this book.

GARDEN ANAHEIM STUFFED PEPPERS WRAPPED IN BACON

Anaheim peppers are the perfect size for stuffing and when they have a great year in the garden, I'm stuffing a lot of them! I made these for my parents years ago and they thoroughly enjoyed them!

▌ INGREDIENTS

6-7 Anaheim peppers about 4-6 inches long

4 ounces cream cheese, softened

1/4 cup Cabot Cheddar cheese, grated, or Dubliner

1/4 cup pepper jack cheese, grated

1/4 cup onion, minced

3 large garlic cloves, minced

1/2 cup cilantro, chopped

3 tablespoons lime juice

1/4 teaspoon chili powder

1/4 teaspoon salt mix

Freshly ground black pepper

6 slices of bacon

Prepare the peppers according to the **note** on the previous page. Line a baking sheet with foil and place a rack on top. Add all ingredients except the peppers and bacon into a small food processor, and pulse blend until consistency is even, and well mixed. **Preheat the oven to 450°F.** Stuff each pepper, tightly packing in the cheese filling. Wrap a bacon slice evenly around each pepper and tuck ends under the bottoms. Place the peppers cheese side up on the rack, and bake for 15-20 minutes, then broil at the end for about 2 minutes more until bacon is to your desired crispness. Keep a close eye at this point so they don't burn.

Note: See my recipe for **boursin cheese spread,** as the boursin cheese may also be used in place of the cream cheese in this recipe.

BOURSIN STUFFED AND BACON WRAPPED HUNGARIAN PETER PEPPERS

This is another one of my favorite peppers to stuff. They are a cross pollination between Anaheim and Peter peppers, and they are a major producer. Since they are the perfect size for stuffing, they make a special appetizer to pass around to your heat loving fans, or go well served alongside a grilled steak, or anything grilled for that matter.

Serves 4-5

▌ INGREDIENTS

9-10 Hungarian Peter peppers or any spicy pepper of choice

1 recipe **boursin cheese spread**

4-5 slices double smoked Niman Ranch bacon, or any bacon, sliced crosswise into about 4 inch pieces

10 wooden toothpicks

Preheat oven to 425°F. Prepare the peppers for stuffing according to the note on the recipe page for sausage and cheese stuffed Anaheim peppers. Line a baking sheet with foil and place a rack on top.

With a small spoon (I saved my kids baby spoons and these are the ones I use for this), stuff the peppers with the boursin cheese spread with just enough to seal peppers. The cheese should hold the pepper when you squeeze the sides together. Wrap each stuffed pepper with a bacon slice and secure with a toothpick. Place on a rack and bake 30 minutes. Some of the cheese will ooze out, and some bacon will shrink up, but its ALL good!

Note: These peppers may also be dipped in egg and then breadcrumbs before rolling in bacon. Use 2 beaten eggs and about 2 cups breadcrumbs. See photo below.

STUFFED PENNSYLVANIA DUTCH HEIRLOOM PEPPERS AKA "FIREBALLS"

My sister Carin gave me the seeds for these peppers and they are incredibly spicy, but so delicious! This stuffing is similar to the boursin cheese dip recipe, but with half the cream cheese.

Serves 2-3 per person, (or as much heat as your mouth can handle!)

▌INGREDIENTS

16 Pennsylvania Dutch heirloom peppers, or any small hot pepper

4 ounces cream cheese, softened

2 ounces crème fraîche

1/4 cup mayonnaise

1 garlic clove, minced

1 teaspoon Dijon mustard

6 large leaves Genovese basil, chopped, about 2 tablespoons

2-3 tablespoons dill, minced

Prepare the peppers for stuffing according to the **note** on the recipe page for **sausage and cheese stuffed Anaheim peppers**.

Preheat toaster oven to 375°F. Line a baking sheet with parchment paper. In a medium bowl, add all the ingredients except the Pennsylvania Dutch peppers. Mix well and stuff the peppers, but not over stuffing. Place all the peppers on the baking sheet as you stuff them. Save the rest of the stuffing for chips or crackers.

Bake in the toaster oven for 15-20 minutes. I like serving these cute peppers on my deviled egg platter. Don't let the cuteness fool you, they live up to their name!

SPINACH BOURSIN STUFFED MUSHROOMS

My mom always made stuffed mushrooms growing up, and she taught me how to sauté the stalks with the onion and garlic for flavor, so as not to waste those precious stems. Sometimes I make these along with the boursin and bacon wrapped Hungarian Peter peppers. It makes for a fun appetizer platter.

Serves 2 per person as a passed hors d'oeuvre or 4 as a dinner side

▌ INGREDIENTS

12 white button mushrooms, cleaned, end of stems thinly trimmed, stems removed and reserved

Drizzle of extra virgin olive oil

1 small onion, finely diced

2 large garlic cloves, minced

Mushroom stems, finely diced

8 ounces frozen spinach, thawed, drained and squeezed dry

1/2 cup boursin cheese spread, room temperature

1/2 tablespoon lemon juice

1/2 teaspoon salt mix

Freshly ground black pepper, added to desired taste

2-3 slices Niman ranch double smoked bacon cut into 2 inch pieces, or any bacon

1/2 cup extra dry vermouth, or water

Spray a light coating of oil on a small baking sheet so the mushrooms don't stick. Remove the stems from the mushrooms by grasping the base, pushing back and forth so it snaps right out. Set the mushroom caps stem side up on the baking sheet and finely dice the stalks. In a medium sauté pan, heat up the olive oil and sauté the mushroom stalks, onions, and garlic. Cook just long enough to soften about 5-7 minutes, then remove from heat and set aside to cool. Add the spinach to a food processor and pulse blend until smooth or chop finely by hand.

Preheat oven to 425°F. In a medium bowl, add the spinach, mushroom stalk mixture, boursin cheese spread, lemon juice, salt, and black pepper. Mix ingredients together, and pile high into the mushroom caps and place each back on the baking sheet. Cut the bacon into uniform pieces and top each mushroom cap with a piece. Pour the vermouth or water carefully around the mushroom caps on the baking tray. Bake for 25 to 30 minutes.

ITALIAN STYLE CLAMS CASINO STUFFED MUSHROOMS

My dad and mom were the king and queen of making clams casino. Dad was the shucker and Mom made the filling. We LOVE it so much, they inspired these amazing mushies.

Serves 2-3 per person

INGREDIENTS

14 medium to large button mushrooms, or cremini, cleaned, stem ends thinly trimmed, stems removed and reserved

Drizzle of olive oil and a tbsp or so of Kerrygold butter

Mushroom stems, finely diced

1 cup red onion, finely diced about 1/2 a large onion

1 cup red bell pepper, finely diced, about 1/2 a large or 1 small

2 tablespoons parsley stalks, minced

3-4 large garlic cloves, minced, at least 2 tablespoons

1 teaspoon dried oregano

Squeeze of lemon juice

1/4 cup extra dry vermouth

8 slices Niman Ranch maple bacon cut into lardons, 1 inch crosswise pieces

1/2 cup extra dry vermouth, or water

Parsley, chopped for garnish

Lemon wedges to squeeze juice on top after baking

FOR THE BREADCRUMB STUFFING

INGREDIENTS

2 cups coarse breadcrumbs from ciabatta bread, or 3-4 slices Udi's grain bread for gluten free

1/2 teaspoon oregano

1/2 teaspoon onion powder

1/4 cup garden parsley

1/4 teaspoon salt mix

Freshly ground black pepper

Preheat toaster oven to 300°F. In a large nonstick skillet, start by slowly browning the bacon and while that's cooking, place the bread slices in the toaster oven, and bake about 10-15 minutes to dry the bread out.

Spray a light coating of oil on a small baking sheet so the mushrooms don't stick. Remove the stalks from the mushrooms by grasping the base and pushing back and forth so it snaps out. Set the mushroom caps stem side up on the baking sheet and finely dice the stalks.

continued ⟶

Meanwhile, in sauté pan set to medium, add the olive oil and the butter. When hot, add the mushroom stalks, onion, bell pepper, parsley stalks, and garlic. Sprinkle with a pinch of salt, freshly ground black pepper and the oregano. Sauté until soft and just taking on some color, then deglaze the pan by adding a squeeze of lemon juice, and the **1/4** cup vermouth. Stir around and when most of the liquid is absorbed, set aside to cool. When bacon is half cooked, using a slotted spoon, remove as many pieces as you have mushroom caps to place on the tops while baking, and set on a paper towel. Continue to cook the rest until browned. When the rest has browned, remove to a bowl lined with paper towels and drain until ready to use.

Take out the bread slices and after cooling slightly, tear into pieces and add to a small food processor. Pulse blend into coarse crumbs. Add the seasonings and pulse blend until just incorporated and the parsley is chopped.

Change the toaster oven temperature to 400°F. or preheat oven to 400°F. In a large bowl, add the breadcrumbs, and mix in the cooled onion and pepper mixture. Chop the drained bacon and mix that in. Taste for seasoning. Stuff mushrooms with the filling and top each one with a slice of the half-cooked reserved bacon. Pour the **1/2** cup vermouth or water carefully around the mushroom caps on the baking tray. Bake 20 minutes, then flip the oven to broil and cook another 5-8 minutes keeping an eye so as not to burn. When done, serve right out of the tray or remove to a serving plate. Sprinkle with lemon juice and parsley and serve.

Note: When picking the blossom, first be careful there isn't a bee hiding inside – they love these! Grab hold of the blossom and snap off just at the bottom at the end of the stem. For preparing the blossoms for stuffing: using a pair of tweezers (specifically for kitchen use), gently open the blossom and remove the single stamen (this is how you know it's a male blossom) by pinching it at the base. This may take a couple of times to get it all out. Pick off the small green leaves on the outside. Under slow running water, give a quick rinse inside and out, and pat onto paper towels to blot off the excess water. Sometimes, I spread the petals and stand them upright to drain, but some aren't so cooperative.

STUFFED SQUASH BLOSSOMS

*These are addictive and once you've had them, you'll be searching for flowers every day. I keep extra filling and batter in the fridge at the ready for when I find new blossoms! Mind you, you won't be feeding a crowd with these unless you're able to get a bunch from the farmer's market, but I generally do 5-8 at a time. This recipe is easily doubled – just taste before adding double salt, as the cheese is already salty. Such crunchy creamy delights they are! Try the **ricotta pancakes** with any extra filling.*

FOR THE BLOSSOMS FILLING
Filling stuffs about 14-26 blossoms.

INGREDIENTS

5-8 garden male squash blossoms, see **note** on previous page

1/2 of a 15 ounce container of organic grass-fed ricotta cheese

1 egg, blended

1/4 cup basil, chopped

2 tablespoons Pecorino Romano cheese

2 tablespoons manchego cheese

1/4 teaspoon salt mix

Freshly ground black pepper

FOR THE BATTER

INGREDIENTS

1/2 cup gluten-free flour, or any flour

1/2 teaspoon salt

Freshly ground black pepper

1/2 cup plus 1/8 cup water, you want a thinner batter

Refined coconut oil for pan frying

Prepare the blossoms for stuffing. Then, in a medium bowl, add all the ingredients except the squash blossoms and mix well. When the blossoms are dry, using a small spoon, gently open the blossom and add about a half tablespoon of the cheese mixture, or more depending on the size of the blossom. I usually fill up to where the petals split. Close and gently twist the blossom closed.

Don't worry if you get a little tear, they still taste great! I also make these substituting all Parmigiano-Reggiano cheese for the Pecorino Romano and manchego cheese.

Once all the blossoms are stuffed, in a non-stick skillet set to medium heat, add a thin layer of oil. When the pan is hot, dip each blossom in the batter dripping off any excess. Sometimes, I brush it against the bowl or use a spoon to scrape off the excess. Add to the pan and brown on each side, about 8 minutes per side. Remove to paper towels to drain and sprinkle with a pinch of salt. Enjoy!

The Grinch

Sauce IT UP

As soon as the herbs roll in, you can bet I begin whipping up some amazing green sauces! I love serving them with all sorts of things, and in late summer, I try saving them all by freezing a few batches for the winter. Let your imagination run free and substitute whatever you have growing in the garden or find at the market, You'll also find a variety of sauces and condiments that accompany the recipes in this book.

GENOVESE BASIL AND CILANTRO CHIMICHURRI

When the herbs are plentiful, and the hot peppers are ripening, there's nothing better than making some chimichurri sauces. True, they may not be totally authentic Argentinian sauces, but they sure are fun to create using a variety of different herbs and vinegars.

▌ INGREDIENTS

2-2 1/2 cups packed Genovese basil leaves, washed and dried

1 cup packed cilantro, washed and dried

1/2 cup extra virgin olive oil

2-4 garlic cloves, 2 large or 4 smaller

1/8 cup lime juice

1/8 cup red wine vinegar

2-3 Thai peppers, seeded and chopped, optional

1 1/4 teaspoons ground cumin

1/2 teaspoon salt mix

Freshly ground black pepper

Add all the ingredients into a large food processor. Pulse blend and add only a **1/4** cup of the olive oil to start. Then scrape down the sides of the bowl and blend in the last **1/4** cup of olive oil through the feed tube. Taste for seasoning. Best made ahead so the flavors have a chance to blend and bring to room temperature for serving.

Note: Chimichurris' are the best for pairing with anything grilled. When having a party or many guests, making a mixed grill with a chimichurri sauce is always a hit.

BASIL MINT CHIMICHURRI

This is another chimi favorite that goes well with anything.

▌INGREDIENTS

2 cups packed basil, washed
  and dried

1/2 cup packed mint, washed
  and dried

1/2 cup extra virgin olive oil

2 hot peppers of choice, seeded
  and chopped

3 garlic cloves

1/4 cup red wine vinegar

1/2 teaspoon ground cumin

1/2 teaspoon salt

Freshly ground black pepper

Blend well in a large food processor. Taste for seasoning. Make ahead so the flavors have a chance to blend and bring to room temperature for serving.

BASIL PESTO

*Pesto is a thicker sauce with less oil than a chimichurri and mostly includes some nuts and cheese and no vinegar. It's origination in Liguria, Italy, pesto is incorporated into many dishes, such as a topping for **bruschetta** and my kid's favorite they grew up with - basil pesto pasta. This is our longtime basic recipe that my son Nolan put in his preschool cookbook. Every summer we make many batches; it freezes well and makes a great easy dinner. When making one batch I like to use the mortar and pestle, but for multiple batches, I use the food processor.*

*Makes about **2/3** cup*

▌ INGREDIENTS

2 cups packed Genovese basil leaves, washed and dried

2 large garlic cloves

1/4 cup extra virgin olive oil

1/4-1/3 cup toasted pine nuts, see **note**

1/4-1/3 cup freshly grated Parmigiano-Reggiano cheese, or Grana Padano cheese

1/2 teaspoon salt mix

Freshly ground black pepper

In mortar, add garlic cloves, salt, and pepper. Using the pestle, mash the garlic until it turns to a paste. Add the basil leaves and begin mashing them by using circular motions against the mortar with the pestle. When starting to come together, add half the pine nuts as well as the olive oil and mash those in. Then add the rest of the nuts keeping a nice chunky consistency. Finally, fold in the cheese with a spatula and taste for seasoning.

Alternately, for multiple batches, use a food processor. Begin by puréeing the basil and garlic. With machine running, drizzle in the olive oil. Stop machine and add in the nuts, salt and pepper, and pulse blend to the consistency you like. We like to have little chunks of the pine nuts. Lastly, add in the cheese and give a quick pulse just to blend. If serving with one pound of pasta, add a little pasta water to the cooked drained pasta before stirring in the pesto. For bruschetta, rub a garlic clove or a half of tomato on your sliced toasted bread of choice. Spoon on some pesto adding chopped tomato, if desired. Sprinkle with extra Parmigiano-Reggiano cheese and bake at 350°F. for about 10 minutes. If freezing the pesto, add to a small container, drizzle olive oil just to cover top and label with date. Or see **roasted tomatoes bruschetta**.

Note: I use a small non-stick skillet to toast pine nuts and the walnuts for the **curly zucchini and cucumber noodles with creamy basil walnut pesto.** On low to medium heat, add in the nuts, tossing about 5-7 minutes until nice and golden, just don't disappear - I 've burned them more times than I care to admit.

HOLY BASIL AND PARSLEY CHIMICHURRI

Holy basil, is a variety of basil also known as Tulsi, and it self-seeds every year and grows all over the garden. It smells incredible and when the purple flowers come out, the bees just love it!

INGREDIENTS

2 cups packed holy basil leaves,
  or any basil

1 cup packed parsley, with stalks

2 large garlic cloves

2 el chaco peppers, or any hot
  pepper of choice

1 teaspoon cumin

1/2 teaspoon salt mix

Freshly ground black pepper

2/3 cup extra virgin olive oil

1/4 cup red wine vinegar

Add first 7 ingredients to a food processor and pulse blend until the consistency is smooth and a bit chunky. Add **1/2** cup olive oil and the vinegar to start. Blend well and stream through the rest of the olive oil through the feed tube. Store in the fridge and bring to room temperature before serving.

LAMBS QUARTERS PESTO WITH CASHEWS

I love this pesto – it is very nutty!

INGREDIENTS

2 cups packed lambs quarters leaves, or spinach

4 garlic cloves

1/3 cup roasted and salted cashews

1/2 cup lightly packed Parmigiano-Reggiano cheese, finely grated

1/2 teaspoon salt mix

Freshly ground black pepper

1/2 cup extra virgin olive oil

In a food processor, start by blending the garlic and the leaves. Add in the cashews and pulse blend. Next, add the cheese, **1/4** teaspoon of the salt to start (The nuts and cheese are salty so add the last **1/4** teaspoon if needed when all done.) and pepper then drizzle the oil with machine running through the feed tube. Great served with any grilled steak and a side of potatoes.

CURLY ZUCCHINI AND CUCUMBER NOODLES WITH CREAMY AVOCADO BASIL PESTO WITH WALNUTS

This makes a nice summer lunch or dinner side dish any time and you can keep it vegetarian by omitting the chicken. If you don't have a spiralizer, a peeler also works well.
*Serves 4 and makes **1 1/2** cups sauce*

▌ INGREDIENTS

2 medium ripe Hass avocados cut into cubes (if too ripe, skip making this dish and make some guacamole)

2 cups soft packed Genovese basil

3/4 cup toasted walnuts, measure whole, see **note** on page 239

4 tablespoons lemon juice

Scant 3/4 teaspoon salt mix

Lots of freshly ground black pepper

1/4 cup plus an 1/8 cup extra virgin olive oil

3 large garlic cloves, large dice

1 small zucchini, spiralized

1 medium cucumber, spiralized, preferably a Japanese or English cucumber as they contain less seeds

3 cups cooked shredded chicken breasts, optional

Begin by measuring out all the ingredients so everything is ready to go. Then, spiralize the zucchini and cucumber and place in a large bowl.

In a food processor, add avocado cubes and then drizzle over the lemon juice. Add basil leaves, garlic, **1/2** teaspoon salt to start and freshly ground black pepper. Pulse to blend. When still a bit chunky, add the walnuts and pulse blend drizzling **1/4** cup of the olive oil through the feed tube. At this point, taste for seasoning adding a pinch more salt and more black pepper and pulse blend the last **1/8** cup of olive oil.

Mix the sauce into the spiralized noodles and add the chicken if desired. Garnish with fresh basil leaves. You really want the lemon to come through, so if you think it needs more, squeeze a bit more on top and serve.

GARDEN FRESH TOMATO SAUCE

*This simple sauce is great for any tomatoes you may have in the garden or find at the market and may be adjusted to as many pounds as you'd like to make. Use with anything you love with tomato sauce, or give it a try on my **chicken parmigiana.***

INGREDIENTS

3 cups tomatoes, seeded and diced

1/2 medium red onion, finely diced

1 tablespoon extra-virgin olive oil

1 large garlic clove

Pinch of oregano

1/4 cup of mixed chopped parsley and basil

1/4 of a red jalapeno or red cayenne pepper minced, optional but give it a try if you like a fra diavolo (spicy) style sauce

1/4 teaspoon salt

Freshly ground black pepper

Sauté the onion and garlic (and the hot pepper if using) in extra-virgin olive oil until soft, then add the tomatoes and simmer for 10-15 minutes stirring a few times to break up the tomatoes. Add in the oregano, pepper and salt and cook a few minutes more.

Blend with an immersion blender for a smooth sauce or leave chunky. Turn out into a bowl and stir in the fresh herbs 5 minutes before serving. Keep warm if serving shortly after making it, or store in the fridge or freezer.

Note: If you find the sauce too thin, feel free to add and simmer in a couple tablespoons of tomato paste and adjust seasonings.

Any of these sauces are terrific on sandwiches and of course any of the fish cakes and burgers. They also make great potato chip and French fry dippers.

CAPER BASIL MAYONNAISE

INGREDIENTS

1 cup mayonnaise

1/4 cup basil, chopped

Juice of 1/2 lemon or more

1 tablespoon capers, chopped

Minced hot pepper if desired

Pinch salt and black pepper

Add all ingredients into a small bowl and mix well. Keep in the fridge until ready to serve.

GENOVESE BASIL AND VIETNAMESE CORIANDER AIOLI

If you don't like eating raw egg, substitute 3/4 cup mayonnaise.

INGREDIENTS

1 egg

1 egg yolk

1 large garlic clove

2 tablespoons lemon juice

1 1/2 teaspoons Dijon mustard

20 basil leaves (3-4 tops)

4 sprigs Vietnamese cilantro or regular cilantro

1/2 teaspoon salt mix

Freshly ground black pepper

1/2 cup grapeseed oil

1/2 cup extra virgin olive oil

Add all ingredients to a small food processor except the oils. When machine is running, drizzle the oils slowly through the top holes, blending about 10 minutes until smooth and creamy. You could also use an immersion blender for this with the cup that comes with it. Keep in the fridge until ready to serve.

ROSEMARY AIOLI

My daughter Cristina came up with this recipe and we love it with burgers off the grill along with a side of hot sauce.

▌INGREDIENTS

1/2 cup mayonnaise

About 1/2 tablespoon fresh rosemary, finely minced

Splash of sherry vinegar

Splash of lemon juice

Freshly ground black pepper

Mix all ingredients in a small bowl. Taste for seasoning and serve with burgers.

Mr. Heat Miser

DID SOMEONE SAY
Hot Sauce?

I absolutely love the beauty of peppers! So much so, I grow anywhere from 85-100 varieties every summer. My obsession started many years ago and continues to grow every year. Not only are their rainbow colors beautiful to look at, their blossoms, varying shapes, and textures make them unique. I find it so fun experimenting with their flavors and colors, and of course, their heat levels. I especially love creating new hot sauces every summer and my family and friends can't get enough of them!

VINEGAR RED HOT SAUCE

*This hot sauce is a must every summer and is particularly great with eggs, fried rice and used in a few of the recipes in this book, such as **General Tso's chicken**, or mix into mayonnaise for a sandwich spread. My kids pour it on everything! These peppers need to ferment which takes a week, to week and a half, so plan ahead if making for something in particular. This sauce is not "blow your head off" spicy, but it has amazing flavor. Makes 20-21 ounces.*

▎INGREDIENTS

1 pound any combination of mixed peppers such as chipotle, red jalapeño, red serrano, hot cherry red, habanero, goat horn, Asian, red devil's tongue, sriracha or sivn

2 tablespoons grey sea salt

ON THE THIRD DAY ADD:

▎INGREDIENTS

1 1/2 cups distilled white vinegar

1/2 cup apple cider vinegar (with the mother such as Braggs)

Using protective gloves, cut off the stems and slice lengthwise removing most of the seeds. I save them so I generally do this part, but it's okay to have some seeds. In a food processor, blend until well mixed but still a little chunky texture. You don't want it liquefied. Place into a ball jar large enough to hold the peppers and eventually, 2 cups of vinegar. Place on the lid and just barely turn – you want the lid to be loose. Place in a cool spot away from direct sun and let sit for 2-3 days. I put a post it right on the jar, so I can keep track of when I started and when I need to finish.

Let sit anywhere from 8-12 days with the lid on loosely. This is what I love about this recipe is that you can finalize it the day you have time, generally between one and a half to two weeks. When ready to bottle, add all to the blender and blend well. With a fine mesh strainer set over a bowl large enough to be steady, add the hot pepper sauce. I like to use my glass quart measuring cup which also makes it easy to pour. Stir and press with a spatula until the remaining peppers are very dry, being sure to scrape the outside of the strainer. Using a funnel, pour carefully into 3 and 5 ounce bottles, or any bottles of choice. Store in the refrigerator.

Note: Try experimenting with different vinegars and salts you like, adjusting the amount of vinegar to weight of peppers, at least 12 ounces to 1 pound or more. With the remaining pulp, I add it to a 16-ounce ball jar and fill with water, then after a few days of steeping, I strain and place in a spray bottle for a natural insect spray for the garden.

RED THAI SRIRACHA SAUCE

Sriracha is a hot sauce that originated in Thailand and we love it on anything! We like making our own as store bought varieties are loaded with stabilizers and preservatives. The spice level of this hot sauce may vary depending on the combination of red peppers used. You may also adjust the ingredients if you have more peppers. I use a mix most of the time, but you could use all one variety.

*Makes 1 4-ounce bottle sriracha, 1 4-ounce bottle spicy toasted sesame oil, and **1 1/2-cup jar Korean Gochujang***

▮ INGREDIENTS

12 ounces mixed spicy red peppers, such as Asian, Thai, goat horn, cayenne, red devil's tongue, sivn, bhut jolokia ghost, Trinidad scorpion, etc.

4 large garlic cloves, sliced in half

2 1/2 tablespoons coconut palm sugar

1 1/2 tablespoons salt mix

1/3 cup distilled white vinegar, or try apple cider vinegar

Using protective gloves, slice the stems off the peppers and cut in half lengthwise. Remove seeds with a small paring knife and keep varieties separate if saving. I am generally a fanatic about getting every seed, but here it's ok if you leave some in there. In a large food processor, add all the peppers, the garlic cloves, sugar, and salt. Pulse to blend keeping a rough chopped consistency. Use your spatula to turn out into a glass ball jar or glass bowl, being careful not to breathe in the pepper fumes especially when you take the lid off the food processor. If I use a ball jar, I turn the lid upside down to cover the top or I use some plastic wrap lightly over the top if using a bowl. Don't seal tightly. Place in a spot out of direct light and let ferment for 3 full days. Check this mixture every day. On the 4th day, add the mixture to a ceramic saucepan or any non-reactive pan and stir in the vinegar. Continue to stir every so often at a low simmer for about 15-20 minutes.

I like to use my 1 quart glass measuring cup with my finest mesh strainer set over the top which makes it easy to pour. Carefully pour the mixture into the strainer and with a spatula, gently push down on the pepper mixture stirring and pushing until you can't get any more liquid. Be sure to scrape down the back of the strainer. Set aside the pulp. Set a funnel that fits your bottle of choice and slowly pour in your Sriracha sauce, scraping every last bit with a spatula. Let cool before capping and placing in the fridge.

SPICY TOASTED SESAME OIL

In another 4 ounce bottle, add 1 tablespoon of the reserved hot pepper pulp from the making of the Sriracha. With a high quality toasted sesame oil, pour it over the paste to fill the bottle. Store in the fridge. I love using this oil to make the **Chinese style vegetable fried rice** and the **Singapore noodle**.

KOREAN GOCHUJANG

This is essentially a chili paste and is by no means an authentic Korean hot sauce, just my take that I make for a friend. The chili pulp stands in for the chili powder.

▌ INGREDIENTS

1/2 cup of remaining pulp from the making of Sriracha

2 teaspoons gluten-free low sodium soy sauce, or any soy sauce

2 teaspoons toasted sesame oil

In a small bowl add the remaining pulp, about **1/2** cup, and sir in the soy sauce and sesame oil. Place in a small jar and store in the refrigerator.

PICKLED PEPPER COINS

Ok, so not a hot sauce, but they are still hot! These peppers may be canned for winter storage or kept in the refrigerator since they get eaten up so fast. For both, you will need 2-pint ball jars with lids and a large pot, if canning. I love these pickled peppers and juice in my **cabin tartar sauce***. They are also fabulous on sandwiches or nachos!*

▌INGREDIENTS

10 spicy banana peppers

2 chipotle peppers

2 jalapeño peppers

2 serrano peppers

3 cups distilled white vinegar

1 cup water

2 large garlic cloves, smashed

2 teaspoons garden coriander seeds

In a medium saucepan, add the vinegar, water, garlic cloves, and the coriander seeds. Bring to a boil then turn down the heat to a gentle simmer for 5-7 minutes. Remove the garlic.

Fill your canner with water that is just high enough to know the jars will be covered. Add the empty jars and lids and bring the temp up to just below the boil but hot enough to sterilize the jars and lids. When jars are sterilized, remove and place to drain on a clean kitchen towel. Sometimes I run mine through the dishwasher ahead of time to omit this step, but either way, the jars need to be hot before adding the liquid.

Meanwhile, thinly slice the peppers into circles removing seeds as you slice. Add all the peppers to a medium bowl and gently mix to evenly distribute the varieties. Keep varieties separate if saving seeds.

Evenly pack the peppers between the jars pushing down gently with a wooden spoon. Pour in the vinegar leaving a **1/2** inch headspace (I leave the space from the bottom rim). Get out the air bubbles by pressing down with a spoon. Gently put on the lid and tighten until just snug. If storing in the fridge let jars cool first. If canning, read on.

With canning tongs if you have them, or a large long handled spoon, place the jars in the water. Bring to a boil, put the lid on and boil for 10 minutes. Make sure it is at a gentle boil so that the water won't boil over. After 10 minutes, remove the lid and let the jars sit in the pot of water for 5 more minutes with the heat turned off, but kept on the burner.

Remove with the tongs, tilting slightly to let water roll off the top and let them cool on the kitchen towel. When you hear the lid pop within a few minutes, the seal is complete. Now you may store them when cooled completely. If you don't hear a pop, the lid has not sealed, so store in the refrigerator and eat this jar first.

HABANERO HEAVEN HOT SAUCE
AKA MY BUFFALO SAUCE

*I almost didn't include this recipe because it contains so many different peppers, but this is my buffalo sauce I use for **buffalo chicken tenders** and **pecan crusted buffalo turkey tenderloins**. Of course, use whatever pepper combos you have, or you could use 10-12 orange habaneros which I always see at the grocery store.*

*Makes two **1/2**-cup jars*

▌INGREDIENTS

3 Caribbean red habanero peppers

6 white bullet peppers

1 Jamaican hot chocolate habanero or black Congo pepper

1 yellow bhut jolokia ghost pepper

2 orange habaneros

1 Monticello fish pepper

1 red bell pepper

1/2 cup about 2 shallots, diced

5 *roasted garlic* cloves

1 tablespoon grapeseed oil

ADD:
▌INGREDIENTS

1/8 cup apple cider vinegar

1 tablespoon sherry vinegar

1/2 tablespoon grey salt

Seed all the peppers and cut into similar sizes. In a large skillet, add the oil, peppers, shallots and garlic. Sauté 20 minutes on low, stirring occasionally, being sure not to let them brown. Add **1/3** cup water (**1/2** cup if you want a thinner sauce) and simmer and stir another 10 minutes or until most of the liquid is gone. Using a spatula, transfer peppers to a high-speed blender.

Monticello Fish Peppers

Place the lid on top and cover the open hole with a folded paper towel taking care not to burn yourself as the liquid will be hot. Blend well and pour into your desired glass jars or bottles. Be careful of the fumes when you take the top off. This is a thicker sauce, so I like to put into jars, plus it makes it easier to spoon out for recipes.

SMOKEY RED CHERRY BOMB PEPPER SAUCE

This hot sauce gets its smoky flavor from the smoked alder salt and tastes incredible with anything hot off the grill. Of course, we also just love it to dip chips!

▊ INGREDIENTS

6 hot red cherry bomb peppers, or hot cherry red peppers

1 orange bell pepper

1 medium red onion

4 garlic cloves

drizzle of grapeseed oil

2/3 cup water

1/3 cup apple cider vinegar

2 tablespoons sherry vinegar

Scant tablespoon smoked alder salt

Seed all the peppers and cut into similar sizes so they cook evenly. Dice the onions and garlic into similar sizes. In a medium sauté pan, add the oil, peppers, onion, and garlic. Stir often on medium low heat so as not to brown. Cook until soft, about 20 minutes. Add in the water and cook until most has evaporated and mixture is very soft.

Carefully transfer all to your blender and add the vinegars and salt. Cover the open hole with a folded paper towel and blend well. Transfer to your favorite bottles or jars and store in the refrigerator.

Ají Amarillo Blossom

Ají Amarillo peppers on the plant.

Kaffir Lime

AJÍ AMARILLO SAUCE

The Amarillo pepper grows about 4-6 inches long and has a fantastic citrusy, fruity flavor with a medium spice level. This sauce is simple to make and freezes well for quick additions to any dish. Try it with the **Peruvian lomo saltado** or with any Mexican dish.

Makes about three 1-ounce jars, scant **3/4** cup

⬧ INGREDIENTS

7 Ají Amarillo peppers, see **resources**

Water to cover peppers when cooking

2 tablespoons reserved cooking water

1/8 teaspoon Peruvian pink salt or grey salt

Cut the stems off the peppers and slice down the middle lengthwise. Take out the seeds leaving the ribs. In a medium saucepan, add all the peppers and cover with water. (Sometimes I add a strip of kaffir lime zest to add more citrus flavor.) Bring to a low boil. Set a timer for 12-14 minutes. Drain the peppers, reserving the liquid.

Place peppers in a bowl and cover with paper towels for about 10-15 minutes. Then, using my mini tongs or a paring knife, peel the skin off the peppers and don't worry if all the skin doesn't come off. Place the peppers in a food processor, add the reserved water and salt of choice. Blend to a nice smooth consistency.

The handwritten label on the bottle reads: Jamaican Hot Choco Haba BBQ sauce

JAMAICAN HOT CHOCOLATE HABANERO BBQ SAUCE

Not only do I absolutely love the color of this BBQ sauce, but I love the spicy sweet flavor and it pairs well with grilled chicken, pork or ribs.

Makes about 20-21 ounces.

▌ INGREDIENTS

10 Jamaican hot chocolate habaneros, seeded and chopped

2 tablespoons Chilean olive oil, or any olive oil

2 cups sweet onion, rough chopped, about one large onion

8 garlic cloves, chopped

1 1/2 cups ketchup (Sir Kensington's)

1/3 cup packed light brown sugar

2 tablespoons cherry jam

2 tablespoons gluten-free Worcestershire sauce, see **my cupboard**

1/2 tablespoon celery seed

1/2 tablespoon sweet smoked paprika

1/2 teaspoon fine grey sea salt

In a medium bowl, add the ketchup, brown sugar, cherry jam or cherry juice, Worcestershire sauce, celery seed, smoked paprika, and sea salt. Stir to mix and set aside. In a large sauté pan, add the oil and bring to medium heat. Add in the onions and hot peppers. Stir and sauté until onions become translucent and peppers are softened, about 15-20 minutes. You do not want to get the onion browned, so if the heat is too high, turn it down a notch or two. Add in the garlic and sauté a few more minutes. Add the bowlful of mixed ingredients and stir well.

Simmer on low for about 10-15 minutes making sure all onions and peppers are soft all the way through. Transfer to a high-speed blender. Put on the top and with a couple paper towels folded into a square, hold that over the hole and blend until smooth and creamy. The liquid will be hot and steaming, so be careful. Remove the paper towel and let the steam escape being sure not to breathe that in. Remove top and carefully transfer to your desired jars or bottles.

Note: These peppers are incredibly spicy. Stand back when stirring on the stove and especially after taking the top off from the blender as the aroma can get you coughing! When grilling, spread on desired protein of choice during the last 10 minutes of cooking time. If you spread the sauce on too early, the sugars will make it burn on the grill.

DRINKS, JUICES, *& Smoothies*

For as long as I have been studying naturopathy, I have been juicing and making smoothies. I have found that the more you make them, the more second nature it becomes when combining ingredients and finding what goes well together. Sometimes a smoothie is all you need to get you going and a juice fills in the blanks when you need a pick me up. Your body will thank you!

TIPS FOR MAKING IT EASY TO MAKE SMOOTHIES:

I love putting a handful of greens in my smoothies, either fresh or frozen. Some favorites are kale, spinach, lambs quarters or dandelion leaves. Collect greens from the yard in the morning, wash and keep them ready to go in the fridge or freeze them in paper bag packets. Make it even easier by buying 10-ounce bags of organic frozen greens.

Most of the time I use coconut water as the liquid for blending and filtered water if I'm out of that. All of my smoothies start with two bananas or more, so I like to keep some frozen in case I don't have any fresh around. I also love them frozen for when I feel like making some non-dairy ice cream like the **mint chocolate chip** or the **banana peach strawberry.** To freeze ripe bananas, peel and cut them in half and lay on a parchment-lined baking sheet and place it in your freezer. When the bananas are frozen, wrap them up in the parchment and store in a zip top bag. Most of the time, if I have an entire bunch fully ripe, I just put the whole bunch unpeeled in the freezer. To peel frozen bananas remove from the freezer and run under warm water. Cut off the top and bottom tips with a serrated knife, then peel from the top to bottom in strips. Break up to add to smoothies.

For freezing any fresh fruit, wash, dry, and peel if necessary, then lay on a baking sheet lined with parchment and put in the freezer. When frozen, wrap up the fruit and store in a zip top bag. I generally like to freeze, blueberries, pineapple and mango. I always keep 10 ounce bags of organic peaches, frozen wild blueberries, cherries, and sometimes strawberries, mango and pineapple. I find that unless you are making them for more than two people several days a week, the larger bags tend get freezer burn, so I stick to the smaller bags.

If I have extra smoothie, I pour it in a blender bottle and keep it in the fridge and then it's easy to just shake up and drink.

TIPS FOR MAKING IT EASY TO MAKE JUICES:

When juicing, you don't want to stop every time you need to add an ingredient. Having all the ingredients washed and cut to the size of your juicer makes it so easy to make a quick juice. It's all the washing and prepping that takes the time!

Because it can be time consuming, I generally make 2-3 different juices at a time, starting with the lightest (green) to brightest (beet). Always use a lemon or lime to help preserve the juice and keep apples from oxidizing. Be sure to juice greens before citrus, as the citrus will extract more from the greens.

Switch up and use a variety of greens. They can be snipped from the garden, rinsed, patted dry and stored in the fridge or fresh harvested. I usually just walk around the yard and pick a variety and juice with whatever I have for fruit and vegetables in the fridge at the time, unless I am making a specific immune juice. But I do like to use whole heads of lettuce, especially romaine, and I can pick up a 3 pack at the grocery, just like I do for my wedge salads. Try adding different fresh herbs. It only takes a small handful to brighten up any juice. Celery, cucumber, ginger and turmeric are some of my favorites to juice, but I also like fennel, asparagus, parsnips and radishes. Grapefruits, oranges, grapes and pomegranates are also nice to have in the fridge for a spur of the moment juice. You'll become a pro at combining things you like!

Store juices in glass jars, pouring very close to the top allowing in the least amount of oxygen. I usually drink one straight away and then store some in the fridge for later, or the next day.

meyer lemon

TRIPLE MINT
CHOCOLATE BANANA SMOOTHIE

*This is an all-time favorite and so good it's hard to break out of the box to make something different, especially when the mint is flourishing in springtime. This is really my basic smoothie recipe that I follow for pretty much every smoothie I make. See **note**.*

Serves 2 or save one for later

▌ INGREDIENTS

3 frozen or fresh bananas

1/2 bag frozen peaches, from a 10 ounce bag

2 large sprigs mint leaves, about 20 leaves, or use all one kind of mint, each sprig has about 10 leaves

2 sprigs spearmint leaves

2 sprigs chocolate mint leaves

2 tablespoons Vega Sport Chocolate protein powder, or any favorite protein powder, see **my cupboard**

2 tablespoons coconut oil

Coconut water up to level of bananas, about 12 ounces

Pinch sea salt, optional (for added minerals)

Drizzle maple syrup, 100 percent pure, about a 1/2 tablespoon

In a high-speed blender, layer bananas cut in half if fresh and if frozen, see **note** on smoothie tips. Add the peaches, mint leaves (I don't worry about tender stalks), protein powder, coconut oil, and the pinch of salt. Pour coconut water up to level of bananas. Add a drizzle of maple syrup and blend well. If too thick, add a little more coconut water. Sometimes I like to keep it thick and eat it with a spoon.

Note: For my basic smoothie recipe, I work in the order of the ingredients above, but substitute different greens and fruit. I always have the 2 bananas, use less of the frozen peaches (or omit), and then add about a cup and a half frozen fruit of choice. I like blueberries, cherries, strawberries, etc. Then I'll put in any greens of choice like dandelions, kale, or any herbs from the yard (if you like cilantro, give it a try with blueberry), and I also love to use broccoli sprouts. Use a scoop of protein powder of choice, the coconut oil and a pinch of sea salt. Then you can add in any vitamins or superfoods you like. Sometimes I add in a tablespoon of hemp hearts, nuts, vitamin C, liquid minerals, collagen powder, then a drizzle of maple syrup or local raw honey. I enjoy the bitter flavor of dandelions, but if they are too bitter for you starting out, add in the maple syrup or honey. Add anything you love!

SOFT SERVE SMOOTHIE

This smoothie is like soft serve ice cream. Eat it with a spoon as is, or use as the base for a smoothie bowl and add on your favorite toppings.

Makes 40 ounces

▌ INGREDIENTS

2 frozen bananas

1 spoonful chocolate bone broth protein powder, see **note**, about a heaping tablespoon, optional (if not, just add 2 scoops of the Vega or your favorite kind)

1 spoonful Vega Sport chocolate protein powder, about a heaping tablespoon

1 cup frozen mango

1 cup frozen wild blueberries

1 cup frozen spinach

2 tablespoons coconut oil

Pinch grey sea salt

1 1/2 cups coconut water

Add all ingredients to a high-speed blender. Blend well until smooth and creamy.

Note: I don't use the scoop that comes with the protein powders, I just use my regular silverware soup spoon. See **resources** for where to find the protein powders.

WATERMELON LIME COOLER

I absolutely love this simple refreshing juice. If using an extra-large watermelon, juice just half unless serving a crowd, in which case juice two limes.

▌INGREDIENTS

1 watermelon

1 lime, peeled

Garnish with any herbs, a lime wedge and a watermelon wedge

Cut the watermelon from the rind and then cut the watermelon into chunks to fit your juicer. Pass all through the juicer, then juice the lime. Taste and add another lime if you wish. Keep chilled until serving. Feel free to add libations!

Note: Sometimes I add a cucumber and a bunch of cilantro to this tasty treat!

SUN TEA AND LEMONADE FOR ARNOLD PALMERS

My boys love Arnold Palmers, so one day I decided to make both tea and lemonade so they could make their own with no added sugar. These actually taste better with each day and are a heck of a lot cheaper than buying bottles of tea. You will need two, **3 1/2** *quart jars, see* **note**.

FOR THE TEA

▌INGREDIENTS

12 tea bags of choice (we like green tea or Earl Grey)

FOR THE LEMONADE

▌INGREDIENTS

3 large lemons cut into 6 wedges, seeds remove (If your lemons are small, use 5-6.)

3 sprigs stevia, from the plant - about 6 leaves per sprig, or honey or maple syrup to taste

2 large sprigs mint

Tie the bags together and then with kitchen string long enough to hang out of the jar, tie a knot around the string of the tea bags. Fill the jar with filtered water to the top.

Add the lemons, stevia, and mint to the jar and fill to the top with filtered water. Place both jars in the sun no less than 6 hours. Store directly in the jars in the fridge and serve all week. Add in a squeeze of maple syrup or raw honey while the lemonade is still warm from the sun if you like it sweeter. If making for a party, it is great made a couple days ahead.

Note: You can find these jars at Bed Bath and Beyond.

CORN SILK TEA

This is a nice treat if you happen to grow some corn or if you can find organic corn at the market.

▍INGREDIENTS

2 ears silver queen corn, or any variety, see note

4 cups filtered water

Cut off the dark silks from the top of the corn. Peel the corn and save the nice, golden silks (save the husks for tamales if you like).

In a small saucepan, add the silks and the water. Bring to a simmer and continue to simmer on low about 20 minutes. Strain and enjoy with a corn husk as a stirrer. This is corny, like my daughter Cristina says, but it is yummy and sweet! So you can enjoy a sweet drink and the health benefits.

Note: Corn silks are anti-inflammatory, diuretic, flush toxins from the liver and kidneys, and contain Vitamin K.

DANDELION TEA

In late spring, I love searching the yard for volunteer lettuces and herbs that seem to pop out of no-where, not to mention an abundance of dandelion flowers just perfect for drying. I try harvesting as many yellow "dandy" flowers as possible to preserve the medicinal properties for tea all year long. See **note** *on next page.*

DRYING THE FLOWERS

Collect and fill a large bowl with dandelion flowers, cutting just below the bud (making sure they have not been sprayed) about 5-6 cups. Rinse well and spin as dry as possible. On 3 baking sheets lined with parchment paper, place each flower stem side down in rows leaving space between each one. Place in the oven at 118 degrees or alternately, use a dehydrator. Set a timer for 10 minute intervals, rotating trays as necessary, keeping a closer eye on them when you see that the flowers are just about dried. Remove when completely dry and let the dandelions air dry on the counter to cool down. Store dried flowers in glass jars, label with the date, and place in a closed dark cabinet.

MAKING THE TEA

All parts of the "lions tooth" are edible, but the flowers make for a pretty tea. In a teapot with a wire mesh basket, add **1/3-1/2** *cup dried dandelion flowers to fill to the top and set aside. This will depend on the size of your dried flowers. In a small saucepan, boil 3 cups water. Pour a* **1/4** *cup of the hot water into the teapot and swirl it around to heat it up. Drain the water and place back the strainer basket full of flowers.*

Pour and fill to the top with the hot water, place the cover on top and let steep 20 minutes or longer. Pour into desired cup and add honey as desired for sweetness. I love the grassy taste of this tea. Leftover tea may be stored in the refrigerator in a glass jar and is refreshing served cold over ice on a hot day.

Note: Dandelions are literal dynamos containing nutrients such as Vitamin A, B and C, but especially high in many minerals such as potassium, calcium, and magnesium. Known as a bitter and diuretic herb, dandelions are an amazing detoxifier and all parts make for a free kidney, and liver cleanser. You may also use the fresh flowers to make tea.

ANTI-INFLAMMATORY POWERHOUSE JUICE

I like to keep these little shots around, especially in fall when so many people seem to be coming down with something, but even in spring when sinus and allergy issues arise. The daikon radish is great for clearing sinuses. Whenever the kids pop in, I'm sure to give them one of these!

Makes 3-4 shots

▌INGREDIENTS

2 large oranges, such as navels, peeled

1 golden beet, peeled

1 lemon with skin, ends trimmed

5 fingers turmeric, peeled

3 hunks ginger, about 1 1/2-2 inches each, peeled

1 hunk daikon radish, about 3 inches quarter size from the smaller end, peeled

Cayenne pepper for shaking on top, optional

Wash and prepare all the ingredients except the cayenne pepper and pass them through the juicer. Pour into a small glass, and sprinkle some cayenne pepper on top, if desired for extra immune boosting and anti-inflammatory power.

nasturtium flower

ORANGE IMMUNE

This is another variation that is incredible and we all absolutely love it. I make this all the time, sometimes with the carrots and sometimes without. If you are just starting out with juicing, add the carrots as it will make it sweeter. Drink a full glass!

🏷 **INGREDIENTS**

10-14 carrots if small, or 6 regular to large size

6-8 mandarin oranges, clementine oranges, or 2 navel oranges, peeled

2 golden beets, peeled with some of the greens, about 8 leaves

1 grapefruit, peeled

1 lemon with skin on, ends trimmed

1 finger turmeric, about 3 inches long

Hunk ginger, about 2-3 inches long

Shake of cayenne, optional

Wash and prepare all the ingredients except the cayenne pepper and pass them through the juicer. Enjoy with a shake of cayenne pepper on top, if desired for extra immune boosting and anti-inflammatory power.

THE KERMIT

Dad loved frogs and whenever I make this, I think of him, so I dubbed it - the Kermit. Plus, my husband buys me many frogs to place in the garden and they always make me smile. This is one of my favorite summer juices and the first one I turn to when the cucumbers are growing 20 inches or more. Feel free to add any green leaves of choice, such as kale, dandelion, or collards. Depending on the size of your cucumber, this juice makes about 32-40 ounces.

▌ INGREDIENTS

1 long Japanese cucumber or English cucumber

1 head celery

1 medium fennel bulb (great for digestion – if I happen to have one on hand, I put it in)

3 green or red apples, with skin, I prefer green because they are more tart

Small handful of fresh mint leaves

Small handful purslane leaves, see **note**

1 hunk ginger about 3 inches long

1 lemon with skin, ends trimmed

1 lime, peeled

After ingredients are washed, run them through the juicer and enjoy. Sometimes I drink a few glasses during the day, or I store in bottles in the fridge.

Note: Purslane, also known as pigweed, is another nutrient packed weed that grows everywhere in the garden and planters and happens to be the highest plant source of omega-3 fatty acids. Purslane is full of fiber and contains many vitamins and minerals helpful for strong vision and bones. Its lemony flavor makes if great just to nibble in the yard, but I also use the whole plant to make tinctures. Its mucilaginous leaves can get gelatinous if you put too many leaves in a juice, but great to thicken a smoothie.

PINEAPPLE CELERY ENZYMATIC ELECTROLYTE

Every year the dill comes up in many containers (because I throw seeds everywhere when the flower turns to seed) on the patio and they are so pretty when they flower. I figured I'd try adding some dill to a juice and I think the flavor of this will surprise you. The enzymes from the pineapple also make this a good drink for digestion.

Makes 1 nice drink, but easily doubled

▌ INGREDIENTS

6 stalks dill, flowers reserved for garnish if you happen to have some

1/2 pineapple, skinned and cut into chunks

1/2 bunch celery, outer stalks

1 lemon unpeeled, ends trimmed

I like to make sure the pineapple, celery, and lemon are cold out of the fridge before juicing this, that way the juice is cold. Run the ingredients through the juicer in the order listed. Garnish with a yellow dill flower, if desired.

ROSÉ LEMONADE

No one can resist this! I used to bring a big jar for my son Nolan every time he had a tennis match and it gave him tons of energy, plus it tastes amazing. It sure beats a Gatorade and it's color is all natural! But if he was home, I would serve it to him in a pretty champagne glass.

▌INGREDIENTS

4 red apples

1 bunch red grapes with seeds

1 lemon, unpeeled, ends
   trimmed

Wash all ingredients and pick the grapes off the vine. Run the ingredients through a juicer and serve, or keep in airtight jars in a cooler if transporting.

MINTY LIME DELICIOUSNESS

This juice drink is an example of what I mean when I say the more you juice, the more you will know what pairs well together. I was randomly gathering herbs and dandelion leaves in the yard, plus I had a few green apples in the fridge, so I put them all together and it became an instant favorite. It's so amazing I think it would make a nice "healthy" margarita mix. Let me know if you test it out!

▌ INGREDIENTS

10-15 stalks parsley

Handful baby dandelion leaves

6 fresh spring mint stalks

3 green apples, unpeeled, stems removed

1 lime, peeled

Wash all ingredients. Bunch all the greens together and run through the juicer first. Then add the lime and then the apples. Enjoy as is or over ice. Garnish with a thin slice of green apple.

CAN'T BEET IT!

Beet juiced with apples is an amazing combo and the color is spectacular. If you need some added iron, this is your drink.

Makes about 3-8 ounce glasses

🚩 INGREDIENTS

1 red beet, on the large side, peeled

6-10 beet green leaves

2 cups red grapes with seeds

2 large red apples

1 lemon with skin, ends trimmed

Wash all ingredients and pick the grapes off the vine. Cut the beet and apples to fit the juicer. Pass all ingredients through the juicer and serve, or store in airtight jars in the refrigerator.

GARDEN HERB JUICE

I like to bring jars of juice out with me while I'm working in the garden and I mostly keep them covered to keep any insects out. Homegrown celery has amazing leaves which are always cut off at the grocery store. I've seen celery with leaves at farmers markets and they add great flavor in salads if you want to try them. Herbs are so packed full of nutrients it's fun experimenting with them in juices, and the ginger and turmeric give this drink a little kick.

Makes 2 small jars full

▌ INGREDIENTS

1 bunch celery, see *note*

Handful garden celery leaves tops

6 large sprigs of parsley with stalks

3 sprigs oregano, about 6 inches long

6 large dandelion leaves or 12 if small

1/2 cucumber with skin

2 large red apples, unpeeled, stem removed

1 lime, peeled

2 inch piece ginger, unpeeled

2 inch piece turmeric, unpeeled

Wash all the ingredients and cut them to size to fit your juicer. Run all the ingredients through and enjoy!

Note: Growing celery from celery is one of my favorite things to do. Plus, it's so much more flavorful and the leaves get huge. To grow your own, cut the bottom end of an organic celery about 3 inches from the bottom end and trim a thin slice off the root. Peel back the outer row of the celery stalks so they snap off. In a small bowl, stand up the celery and pour water just under the top and as it drinks up the water, keep adding more.

In about a week, the stalks start growing from the middle and white roots appear at the base. When the center growth is about 2-3 inches, plant your celery in some good soil covering the celery parts, leaving the new growth above the soil. Kids love doing this!

ANTIOXIDANT PINK JUICE

This is a dream in a glass. Delicious!

⚑ INGREDIENTS

2 large pomegranates

1 large navel orange, peeled but leave on the pith

1 lemon, unpeeled, ends trimmed

Carefully cut and peel the pomegranates, exposing the seeds and gently peel them into a bowl. When all ingredients are ready, juice the pomegranate seeds first, then the lemon and finally the orange. If you have any leftover you may want to hide this one in the fridge!

MINT CHOCOLATE CHIP
ICE CREAM

Okay, so I classify this as a thick smoothie bowl! I don't know whoever came up with "nice" cream for non-dairy ice cream made with frozen bananas, but I must say, having some on hand lends to some quick cravings and mine, aside from potato chips, is mint chocolate chip ice cream. If I had jimmies, I would have put those on top too!

Serves 1-2

▌INGREDIENTS

3 frozen bananas

1/4 teaspoon spirulina

30-40 fresh mint leaves from the garden, about 4 large sprigs

1-2 tablespoons dairy free chocolate chips or your favorite chocolate chips

In a high-speed blender, add all ingredients except chocolate chips and blend until creamy using the tamper. Use a spatula to scoop into a bowl and stir in the chocolate chips or sprinkle on top.

BANANA PEACH STRAWBERRY ICE CREAM WITH BASIL

Another thick smoothie bowl "nice" cream that is refreshing and filling.

Serves 2

INGREDIENTS

2 1/2-3 frozen bananas

1/2 of a 10 ounce bag frozen peaches

1/2 of a 10 ounce bag frozen strawberries

2 tops basil leaves, about 12-14 leaves

1/4 cup coconut water

In a high-speed blender, add all ingredients and blend until creamy using the tamper. Use a spatula to scoop into a bowl and garnish with a basil leaf.

Inspector Poirot from Agatha Christie

Miscellaneous

This section is filled with helpers that go with many recipes in the book, plus some extra delights. You will also find a few of my tips for preserving peppers and herbs. The homemade breadcrumbs come from years of making my own, but here, the following recipes are all utilizing gluten-free bread, so everyone may enjoy dishes including them, and I promise they are delicious! But know you may also use the same recipes substituting your favorite bread, such as ciabatta, or a hearty white farmhouse bread.

GLUTEN-FREE
ITALIAN SEASONED BREADCRUMBS

*This is a great general Italian seasoned breadcrumb. Perfect for the **chicken parmigiana** or for anything requiring breadcrumbs.*

Makes enough for 6-8 breasts with about 1 cup left to freeze

🔖 INGREDIENTS

1 loaf Udi's grain bread, the smaller loaf (they have a long loaf now), see my cupboard

4 Udi's white hamburger buns, separate each into 2 pieces

ADD IN:

2 teaspoons onion powder

2 teaspoons garlic powder

Large handful fresh parsley, basil or both

1 1/2 tablespoons dried oregano

1 tablespoon salt mix

Tons of freshly ground black pepper

As much as you can fit in your toaster oven or oven in one layer, toast the bread lightly. If you toast too dark, the bread gets too hard and makes it harder to blend into crumbs. And be careful, gluten-free bread is finicky, and the pieces get so hot! They also have a lot of moisture which you will notice as you toast the bread. When all the bread is lightly toasted, lay out a long paper towel and teepee the bread 2 slices at a time to cool. Do this with the remaining bread (I usually don't use the heels).

When all the bread is cooled, rip the bread in to pieces and place in the bowl of a large food processor, about 4-5 slices at a time. Pulse and blend well. Transfer each batch to a large bowl and on the last batch of crumbs before blending:

Blend this well and add to the large bowl of crumbs and mix well. You could also use fresh garlic instead of powdered. If you notice larger pieces of breadcrumbs, scoop out with a spoon and put back in the food processor and pulse blend again, then add back to the large bowl. Let the crumbs sit uncovered an hour or so stirring occasionally to let them dry out a little, then store in a covered container. They also freeze well.

ALTERNATE GLUTEN-FREE ITALIAN SEASONED BREADCRUMBS

Another version making a smaller batch of breadcrumbs for things like adding to the fish cakes, **zucchini fries,** *or* **the stuffed chicken breasts with spinach**.

▌ INGREDIENTS

8 slices Udi's grain bread (not the sandwich bread that says our best bread ever – use the original grain)

ADD IN:

1 teaspoon onion powder

1 teaspoon garlic powder

3 tops fresh basil

few sprigs of dill

2 teaspoons dried oregano

1 teaspoon salt mix

Lots of freshly ground black pepper

Preheat toaster oven to 325°F. Place the bread in the toaster oven, directly on the rack. Bake about 10-12 minutes. When all the bread is lightly toasted, lay out paper towel and teepee the bread 2 slices at a time to cool. Do this with the remaining bread.

When all the bread is cooled, rip the bread in to pieces and place in the bowl of a large food processor, 4 slices at a time. Pulse and blend well. Transfer first batch to a medium bowl and on the last batch of crumbs before blending:

Blend this well and add to the bowl of crumbs and mix well. If you notice larger pieces of breadcrumbs, scoop out with a spoon and put back in the food processor and pulse blend again, then add back to the bowl. Let the crumbs sit uncovered an hour or so stirring occasionally to let them dry out a little, then store in a covered container.

GLUTEN-FREE PANKO BREADCRUMBS

Panko are those amazing Japanese breadcrumbs that have such a great texture and crunch. These are great crumbs for just about anything!

Makes 5 1/2 cups

INGREDIENTS

10 slices Udi's grain bread, or 8 plus a hamburger bun (other options are using 1 small loaf Udi's grain bread and 1 bag Udi's white hot dog buns), see **note**

1 1/2 teaspoons salt

Freshly ground black pepper

Preheat oven to 300°F. Rip the bread in to pieces and place in the bowl of a large food processor, about 5 pieces of bread at a time. Pulse bread until blended into uniform crumbs. Turn out onto an extra-large baking sheet and spread evenly. Bake for 10 minutes and then toss the crumbs with a spatula, breaking up those sticking together. Put back in the oven another 8-10 minutes until turning golden on the edges. Toss again with a spatula and let cool on the tray. Crumbs should be nice and golden, and you will hear their crispness when they are done when you shake the tray.

When the crumbs have cooled, return them in batches back to the food processor. Pulse to blend to a panko crumb consistency. You do not want to over blend into a powder. Store in the fridge if using in the next couple of days. They also keep well in the freezer.

Note: This version shows how to make some breadcrumbs with whatever types of gluten-free bread you have, such as hot dog buns, hamburger buns or sandwich bread. Keep in mind the only gluten-free bread I use is Udi's. It's a nice way to use up the extras and sometimes if the kids have come and gone and I have a bunch of different breads that would just end up going bad, I just make the crumbs. Then I have some in the freezer at the ready, making it easy to prepare anything needing breadcrumbs when a special request comes in.

GLUTEN-FREE ITALIAN STYLE PANKO BREADCRUMBS

*I love these particular breadcrumbs for my **arancini di riso**...but they coat anything nicely!*

INGREDIENTS

1 12-ounce Udi's loaf white sandwich bread (I don't use the heels.)

1 1/2 teaspoons onion powder

1 1/2 teaspoons garlic powder

1 1/2 teaspoons dried oregano

Handful of any fresh herbs such as parsley or basil (try lavender or rosemary for a French style Herbs de Provence breadcrumbs)

1 1/2 teaspoons salt

Freshly ground black pepper

Preheat oven to 300°F. Rip the bread in to pieces and place in the bowl of a large food processor, about 4 pieces of bread at a time. Pulse bread until blended into uniform crumbs. Turn each batch of crumbs onto an extra-large sheet pan and spread evenly. Bake for 8 minutes, toss the crumbs with a spatula, bake for 8 more minutes. Toss again and then bake a final 5 minutes. Keep an eye on them at this point so they don't burn – each oven varies. Crumbs should be nice and golden and you will hear their crispness when they are done when you shake the tray.

When crumbs have cooled, return them in batches back to the food processor. Pulse to blend to a panko crumb consistency. Add in the rest of the ingredients and pulse blend to mix. Do not over blend.

ROASTED GARLIC

*Roasted garlic is one of those small touches that gives a nice sweet nutty flavor to many dishes. Of course, it is great just smeared on a piece of bread, but I like to add it to hot sauces, dressings, and potatoes. My mom gave me this awesome garlic roasting dish but I also roast it in parchment-lined foil like I do the onions for the **German potato salad.***

▌INGREDIENTS

4 heads garlic

2 tablespoons extra virgin olive oil, no need to measure just drizzle on

Handful of fresh thyme

Sprig of rosemary

Pinch salt mix

Freshly ground black pepper

Preheat oven to 350°F. Carefully trim the root end bottoms of each garlic head removing any dirt. Slice off about a **1/4** inch of the top exposing the fresh garlic (save little tips for some of the salad dressings). Gently peel off a couple layers of the skin but keep the bulb intact.

On a roasting dish, place the garlic heads on top of the bunch of thyme. Top with the rosemary sprig, drizzle the olive oil and sprinkle with the salt and pepper. Cover the roaster and roast for 1 hour and 20 minutes. Turn off oven and keep in another 10 minutes.

Cool before storing in the fridge. Keeps well to add to recipes through the next 2 weeks. To use, just squeeze the clove from the bottom and it will pop right out. I also like saving the liquid for dressings.

PAN FRIED DANDELION FLOWERS

*I'm not kidding when I say we eat every part of the dandelion! You will not believe how good these are. They make awesome tasty bites served like croutons in a salad or as a garnish to decorate any dinner dish like the **Caesar meatball wedge salad**.*

▌ INGREDIENTS

20 yellow dandelion flowers, rinsed well and spun dry

1 egg, blended

1/4 gluten-free flour, or any flour

1/4 teaspoon chili powder

1/4 teaspoon salt mix

Freshly ground black pepper

Olive oil for pan frying, grapeseed oil or coconut oil

Pour just enough oil to coat a small pan, preferably cast iron or non-stick skillet. In small bowl, blend the egg and in another small bowl, mix together the flour, chili powder, salt and pepper. Dip each flower into the egg and then coat well with the flour mixture, shaking off excess.

When the oil is hot enough, place the flowers in the pan being sure not to crowd them. Pan fry in batches. Keep an eye on the heat so they don't burn – they only take about a minute on each side. Using 2 forks to flip and remove from the pan makes it easy for the oil to drip off. Transfer to paper towel-lined plate to drain then place in a single layer in a serving dish, or top a salad in place of croutons. Serve immediately.

Note: When I know I'm making these, I try to wash and dry them earlier in the day. If the flowers are damp, they won't be as crispy.

HOMEMADE BUTTERMILK

*I can't tell you how many times I've needed buttermilk, but it's just not something I keep on hand, and when you want chicken tenders, you want **chicken tenders**! I'm pretty sure the first time I needed it and didn't have any, I went to my go to, Better Homes and Gardens New Cookbook, and looked up an emergency substitution. Their recipe included whole milk which I never had either, so I used the half-and-half in the fridge that was always there for coffee, and I use double lemon juice because I love lemon. It has been the way I make it ever since. This is the easiest thing to whip up when you need it and I actually like it better than store-bought because it is thicker. Try it also with my **baked fried chicken** or **baked onion rings**. Anyway, can I really call it homemade? I didn't make the half-and-half, but I may have grown the lemons!*

▌ INGREDIENTS

1 cup half-and-half

2 tablespoons lemon juice

Mix the 2 together and store in the fridge. May be made last minute or a day ahead and recipe doubles or triples easily.

SPICY SWEET BACON STRIPS

These are so good with the ricotta pancakes! I even took them to a Washington Nationals baseball game to munch on with friends and they loved them so much they were more than happy to take home what was left.

▌ INGREDIENTS

1 pack Niman Ranch bacon cut in half crosswise

2 1/2-3 tablespoons *vinegar red hot sauce*, or your favorite vinegar based hot sauce

1/2 cup light brown sugar

Preheat oven to 400°F. Marinate the bacon in the hot sauce at least 2-4 hours or overnight. Line 2 baking sheets with parchment (bacon will be transferred to the second baking sheet after 15 minutes of cooking to get the strips out of the fat.) Line bacon on the parchment and place in oven for 15 minutes.

Remove from oven and with tongs, transfer the bacon to the next ready baking sheet (This gets rid of the grease so they don't burn when you add the sugar.) Sprinkle each piece with brown sugar. Place back in the oven for 5 minutes making sure the bacon isn't burning. It's ok if all the sugar doesn't melt. When done, remove and drain on paper towels and serve in a bowl.

RICOTTA PANCAKES

*These make great little hors d'oeuvres served with the **spicy sweet bacon strips**. Bring the two out at cocktail hour and see everyone's eyes light up!*

▌ INGREDIENTS

1/4 cup to 1/2 cup soppressata or pepperoni, finely diced, see **note**

1 recipe squash blossom filling, or the remainder from stuffing the blossoms, see **stuffed squash blossoms**

Coconut oil for pan frying

Mix the soppressata or pepperoni into the filling. With a non-stick pan on medium heat, add enough coconut oil to make a thin coating and drop mixture by 2 tablespoons into the hot pan. Just like cooking pancakes, when you start seeing little bubbles, it's time to flip to the other side, about 3 minutes per side. If pan gets too hot, turn down a notch so they don't burn.

Note: I usually serve these along with the stuffed squash blossoms, so when I make these pancakes, I use the remainder of the filling and add **1/4** cup diced soppressata (an Italian dry salami), or pepperoni to the mixture. If making the entire batch of filling just for these pancakes, then add **1/2** cup. Also, when I use pepperoni, I dice it and then pan fry for about five minutes first to release some fat. Then drain, cool, and add to ricotta mixture.

Bay Leaf Plant

BAKED BACON

*As soon as the first ripe tomato is spotted on the counter by my husband, look out! It's BLT time! Cook up a batch of this bacon for breakfast or use for any **wedge salad**, or try it with my **BLG sandwich** and the **open face BLTP sandwich**.*

INGREDIENTS

1 pack Niman Ranch maple cured bacon, or any of your favorite bacon, see **note**

Line a baking sheet with parchment paper so that it goes up the sides of the baking sheet.

The trick is to place the bacon in the oven even before it has reached the desired 400° on the middle rack. This helps release some of the fat slowly and keeps the bacon from curling up.

Preheat oven to 400°F. Bake for 20-23 minutes or to your desired doneness. Remove each strip of bacon with tongs to paper towels to drain and pat off the grease. Let the grease cool and then slide the parchment right into the trash.

Note: Cooking up 3-4 slices in a pan drove me nuts, but I also didn't like the mess baking it on racks or foil in the oven as the grease always went through. So I lowered the heat and tried parchment paper and it works so well and keeps the grease from going through to the pan. Lay the strips of bacon in a single layer.

Note: Niman Ranch bacon is thicker than most bacon, so adjust your cooking time for the thickness of your bacon.

PRESERVING GARDEN HERBS

From spring to fall, I am continually preserving herbs for cooking, for medicinal purposes, for tinctures and teas. I just love herbs! I find it so relaxing and peaceful to be in the yard trimming back herbs for drying or collecting fresh herbs to use in the kitchen and the fragrances will make anyone smile!

DRYING GARDEN HERBS

Usually, I pick the herbs in the morning when they are full of their medicinal properties. I rinse with the hose or bring in the kitchen to wash. I gather the herbs by their stalks and with kitchen string, I tie the bundle together. I have a long branch fallen from a tree that I use specifically for drying my herbs. I tie the bundles to the branch and balance between two patio chairs and let the herbs dry all day in the sun. At the end of the day I bring them in the house and do the same on two dining chairs. Alternately, I hang them individually under the umbrella of the patio table.

When the herbs are completely dry, I spread a sheet of parchment paper on the counter. Working with one bundle at a time, cut the string off the stalks and take each stalk and run your fingers down letting the crumbled leaves fall onto the parchment, returning the stalk to the compost. When the bundle is done, assess the size jar you will need to store the herb and pick up the parchment and let the herbs slide directly into the jar.

FREEZING FRESH HERBS

Aside from making pestos and sauces that I also freeze, see **sauce it up**, I love to collect fresh herbs, blend them, and freeze in ice cube trays to add to smoothies, soups or sauces during the winter. Wash and dry selected herbs – I particularly love basil, mint, and parsley. Add the herb of choice to a food processor. If I am blending for smoothies, I will add about a tablespoon of coconut oil just to be able to blend. Add more if necessary. Then I portion into ice cube trays and freeze. Once frozen, add the cubes to a parchment bag and store in a zip top bag. If I am doing savory for soups, like basil or parsley, I will add a drizzle of olive oil and do the same with the ice cube trays and freeze. Label the bags as it's hard to tell which is which through the parchment.

I also freeze greens, such as kale, collard greens, and dandelion leaves. Wash the leaves and dry on towels. Lay flat between parchment paper in a zip top bag. Remove leaves as desired to add to smoothies. I also freeze Thai basil and Genovese basil like this for adding to some Thai dishes and mayonnaises during the winter. The leaves turn dark, but all the flavor is there, and when you crave **Singapore noodle** or **basil mayonnaise** for fish cakes in the middle of winter, you'll be glad you froze some!

Bishops Crown Peppers

PRESERVING GARDEN HOT PEPPERS

*Preserving peppers makes it easy throughout the year to use them in a variety of ways and having a box of kitchen gloves comes in extremely handy when handling hot peppers. Aside from pickling, canning, or making hot sauce, see **did someone say hot sauce?**, here are more ways to preserve your peppers.*

FREEZING PEPPERS WHOLE

I found that freezing the peppers retains the heat and flavor. Wash and dry your peppers thoroughly. I generally let them air dry completely on towels on the counter. Place the peppers in a parchment bag and then into a zip top bag, getting as much air out as possible. Try separating peppers and adding about two to three varieties per bag, such as jalapeño and serrano in one bag for quick guacamole anytime, or Asian pepper varieties in another bag. Using a permanent marker, label the outside of the bag with the variety and date.

One thing to note, when you need a pepper, remove from the bag and be sure to cut it within a minute of taking it out of the freezer while it is still semi-frozen. Otherwise, it will be too mushy to cut easily even though it has all the flavor. Cut the stem end off, slice lengthwise and the seeds come right out. I do not save seeds from the freezer peppers.

FREEZING PEPPERS IN ICE CUBE TRAYS

If you have time to prepare a couple trays like this, it is so worth it, and makes it so easy to choose a pepper for a specific dish since the seeds have already been removed, you can mince immediately. My son Nolan loves taking a tray with a variety of peppers to cook with at school.

First, wash and dry the peppers. Cut off the stem end, slice lengthwise and remove the seeds to a small plate or bowl to save. I put a small sticker with the pepper variety right on the plate and move it to another area while doing another variety of peppers. You'd be surprised how seeds go flying and you want to keep them separate.

As you seed the peppers, place by halves or cut into three to four pieces and place in an ice cube tray section. Do this with different varieties until full. On a large post-it, diagram the tray and write down the varieties in each cube slot and keep this handy for when you want to pick a pepper for a certain dish. Place the tray on a piece of parchment large enough to wrap over the top. Then do the same with heavy duty foil. Place in the freezer and use peppers as needed, being sure to rewrap tightly when placing the tray back into the freezer.

Red Devils
Tongue
2017

Amarillo
Yellow
Cayenne
Lemon peps

Westland/
Bishops
crown
2017 peps

Guajillo

DRYING PEPPERS

Drying peppers is an awesome way to make your own chili powders. Like freezing, I dry some whole and also dry some seeded and halved. You'd be surprised how fast the little ones dry on their own right on the counter. Otherwise, I use my dehydrator at 115°. When it gets crazy and I have too many peppers, I dry them whole.

Prepare the peppers by washing and drying well. Seed the peppers and cut lengthwise placing similar sizes on each tray. I keep a note pad next to my dehydrator jotting down the varieties on each tray. Again, label the variety as you go. (I always would say oh, I'll remember and then of course forget and those seeds would end up in a mystery pepper bag!) Place the tray or trays in the dehydrator. Check the dehydrator after 12 hours and see how the peppers are drying. Remove those that are done, cut ones dry faster than whole, and set on paper plates for a day or two to ensure they are completely dry before storing. Write the variety directly on the paper plate. I like to use glass jars to store different varieties but store large amounts into reusable zip top bags. Again, label each bag with a permanent marker. Mince these peppers up in any dish you want some spice, use whole dried peppers in **General Tso's chicken** or see below for making chili powder.

MAKING CHILI POWDER

You will definitely need a mask (Home Depot) for this and also a spice grinder (Amazon) used specifically for hot peppers. I keep two spice grinders, one for hot peppers and one for spices.

When peppers are completely dry, add to the spice grinder. Seeding before drying makes this step that much easier, but if using whole peppers, with gloved hands, break off the stem and crack the pepper in half, shaking the seeds out into a small bowl. Don't worry if you leave one or two behind. If I'm making chili flakes used for a pizza topping, I leave more seeds in and blend to flake size. Otherwise, I blend to a fine powder. Using a small spoon and spatula, carefully transfer to a small glass container. I like to blend single varieties to have taste tests and then I like to make my own blends of chili powders. The colors alone are amazing! My kids sprinkle these on everything!

SAVING SEEDS

I save seeds for everything! When it comes to planting a garden, it's fun to have your own collection and having seeds to share. I also love ordering new varieties of seeds every couple of years and save organic seeds from vegetables and fruits from the grocery or farmer's market.

Many plants in the yard, especially greens, herbs and lettuces will flower, bolt and turn to seed, especially when the temperatures get hot. I let the hardy plants go to seed so that I can collect those. The dill and parsley seeds I simply cut the stalk and save the entire seed flower in a bag, but I'm sure to sprinkle some everywhere first!

For the bulk of my seed collecting, I use small bowls, container tops, or small plates and place stickers right on them labeling with the variety. Leave the seeds out to air dry for at least a week or more to make sure they are completely dry. Store in snack size zip top bags or small envelopes. Use a spoon to scrape the seeds of hot peppers off whatever they are drying on straight into the bag because they are hot and will make your fingers burn.

For saving tomato seeds, I do not do the whole fermenting thing. Using a small knife to get the seeds out of the tomato, I place the seeds on a folded paper towel. Using a butter knife, drag it across the seeds which releases the pulp from the seed and gets soaked up in the paper towel. Transfer with the knife to another paper towel if there is still pulp on the seeds. Keep spreading the seeds over the paper towel until they are clean and when done, transfer them to parchment paper or wax paper to dry. Use a marker to write the variety directly onto the parchment paper. Place in a spot to allow the seeds to dry over the course of a few days to a week. The parchment paper allows the seeds to slip right off when dry, directly into snack size zip top bags or small envelopes.

Then, in a shoebox, I alphabetize the peppers, then the tomatoes, and then the vegetables, citrus and fruits. Label the box with the year. I still have seeds from 2006! Every year, it's fun experimenting to see if seeds will grow and it always amazes me how some sprout from so long ago.

RESOURCES

Amarillo paste and sauce
Amazon.com

Avocados
Avocadoorganic.com

Butters – Tuscan, truffle and other specialties
Lobel's of New York
Lobels.com

Cedar Papers
Amazon.com
Whole Foods Markets

Environmental Working Group
The dirty dozen and clean fifteen foods
Ewg.org

Free Food and Medicine: Worldwide Edible Plant Guide
The most comprehensive book I have ever found on wild edibles and plants.
by Markus Rothkranz
Amazon.com

Kitchen Gloves - non latex
Amazon.com
Costco

Knives
Williams Sonoma

Korean Gochugaru chili flakes
Mother in Law's

Meats
Truly the finest Meats, Seafood and more
Lobel's of New York
Lobels.com

Olive Oil
Fresh Pressed Olive Oil Club - This is the club I get my oils from - the absolute best olive oils! You won't believe the difference in a salad and in all your recipes.
freshpressedoliveoil.com

Protein Powders
The brand I use the most is Vega and is all plant-based. I love both the chocolate and French vanilla All-in-One Shakes. Plus they have a wide variety of mixes for sports performance. I find them at Whole Foods Markets or myvega.com
For adding collagen, I use Dr. Kellyann's SLIM Bone Broth protein powder, great for those who follow a paleo diet. drkellyann.com

Seafood
Lobel's of New York
Truly the finest Meats, Seafood and more
Lobels.com

Seeds
Aside from being a huge seed saver, every couple of years I like to grow new things and add to my collection. I do try different organic and organic heirloom seed places once in a while, but the following are loyal favorites. For Asian seeds of all kinds, I love kitazawaseed.com (also non-GMO) and evergreenseeds.com. Heirloomseeds.com and Monticello shop has a wide variety of heirloom seeds. For medicinal seeds that are open-pollinated and non-GMO, you will enjoy strictlymedicinalseeds.com. For hot peppers, you can't go wrong with superhotchiles.com (refining fire chiles) or pepperjoe.com.

Scan Pans
Nonstick cookware from Denmark
Sur la Table or Amazon.com

Wild Seafood and Organics
Vitalchoice.com

dill flower gone to seed

THANK YOU

First and foremost, this is a book about family. My beautiful children and wonderful husband, my lifelong friends and my professional family who helped make this dream a reality, and, of course, my amazing family of Instagram followers who have supported me from my first-ever post, onward. This includes:

Cristina, Calvin and Nolan, my children, my biggest inspirations and best teachers. Thanks for your endless time spent in the garden, even during those times when you'd likely prefer to be elsewhere. You are my heart! I loved cooking with you when you were growing up and cherish the times we get to cook together now. I am so proud to have seen each of you cook for yourselves in college – you are all amazing in the kitchen. I am so blessed to be your mom! Thank you Calvin for taking the pictures of me in the garden.

Roby, my husband of 29 years. Thanks for working your tail off so I could be home to take care of our kids, thanks for being a great Dad, and making our yard an oasis with your beautiful flowers. And yes, there's gravy with that!

My parents, Fran and Marilyn Cataldo. Most importantly, I want you to know how much it has meant the world to me to be raised by such loving, caring parents. I have grown to learn and do so many things for my children because of the values and respect you both taught me, and that family comes first. Dad, I knew you were always so proud of me and excited for my cookbook, I'm only sorry you aren't here to see it; however, I know you have always been with me in my heart. Nothing made me happier than showing you around the garden and cooking for you any chance I got. Mom, thanks for teaching me by example and being my biggest supporter in life. I'm so glad you made me wash lettuce, scrub mushrooms and weed the garden. As a grandmother, you are more than special to us all. There are no words to tell you how much I love you.

My sister Carin and brother Fran. I love you so much – what in the world would I do without you guys?! Same goes to my fabulous sisters in law, Andrea, Searcy and Alix - and my brothers in law, Norm, John and Eef. We've made many memories all cooking and eating together over the years. And to my sweet amazing nephews, nieces and godson Frannie, I love you guys!

Aunt Angie and Uncle Joe. You have been there for me since day one. What would life had been like without the cabana and all your amazing cookouts and get togethers?! Love and thanks to you both.

My fabulous aunts, uncles, and cousins. You made cookouts and holidays a blast and I love you all. For those who encouraged me to write this book – thank you!

My amazing Father-in-law, Roby, and his love, Libby. You have done so much for me and our family and I am so grateful. Your excitement for me writing this cookbook kept me going on numerous occasions, and I love you loads.

Kelly McConnell, my bestie since the 8th grade. You rock it girl and I couldn't live without you! Thank you for always being a huge inspiration in my life. Thanks too for always making me laugh and for being the real deal! Hugs Matt and my goddaughter Sophie I love you all.

Norma Grose, my BFF for 30 years. Thank you for always having a listening ear. Your wisdom and "keep the faith Kimmer" have kept me going more times than I could ever count, and I love you more than you will ever know. Thanks for always having a seat at my table and sharing our lives together.

My foodie buddies, Sara and Stan, Holly, Scott and Lydia, Jan, and Sam. I'm so glad you share my love of food. Dining out and celebrating all our birthdays throughout the year is a blast. I treasure those times and all of you. Special thanks Jan for being the start to getting me organized by printing out all my pictures. And Sammy D – it wouldn't have been the 4th of July without you sitting in the kiddie pool all those years the kids were growing up.

Dr. Janet Starr Hull, my mentor, friend, and true anchor. Thank you for inspiring me to hit the books so many years ago and for always being there for me and the kids, I love you! Your endless talents never cease to amaze me.

Allison and Graeme. Thanks so much for your friendship and ideas along the way.

Lou Fisher. Many thanks for your help with editing the book and for your many thoughtful ideas and suggestions. So glad we are friends and neighbors!

The LM Marketing Team. Your fabulous vision, direction, and oversight helped bring out the fun in my cookbook and website. I am empowered by all you ladies!

Lastly, my Instagram friends. I have met so many wonderful people! I appreciate everyone who has engaged with me, inspired me, and joined me in my love for the beautiful world of gardening and fabulous food. This book is for you.

In closing, this is a big thanks to ALL who were instrumental in getting me to write this book. And thanks to the many pollinators that visit our yard and garden – whom without, there would be no glorious food.

If you have any questions with any of the recipes or gardening, I'll answer to my ability, I'm just an email away!

Grazie and much love,
Kimmy

INDEX

RECIPE INDEX

KITCHEN CONVERSIONS

CUPS	OUNCES	MILLILITERS	TABLESPOONS
1/16 cup	0.5 oz	15 ml	1 tbsp
1/8 cup	1 oz	30 ml	3 tbsp
1/4 cup	2 oz	59 ml	4 tbsp
1/3 cup	2.5 oz	79 ml	5.5 tbsp
3/8 cup	3 oz	90 ml	6 tbsp
1/2 cup	4 oz	118 ml	8 tbsp
2/3 cup	5 oz	158 ml	11 tbsp
3/4 cup	6 oz	177 ml	12 tbsp
1 cup	8 oz	240 ml	16 tbsp
2 cup	16 oz	480 ml	32 tbsp
4 cup	32 oz	960 ml	64 tbsp

FAHRENHEIT	CELSIUS
200°	93°
250°	121°
300°	150°
325°	160°
350°	180°
375°	190°
400°	200°
425°	220°
450°	230°
500°	260°

IMPERIAL	METRIC
1/2 oz	15 g
1 oz	29 g
2 oz	57 g
3 oz	85 g
6 oz	170 g
8 oz	227 g
10 oz	283 g
13 oz	369 g
15 oz	425 g
1 lb	453 g

SCOVILLE HEAT SCALE

The Scoville scale measures the pungency or heat of peppers and chilis in terms of their capsaicin levels.

HOTTEST

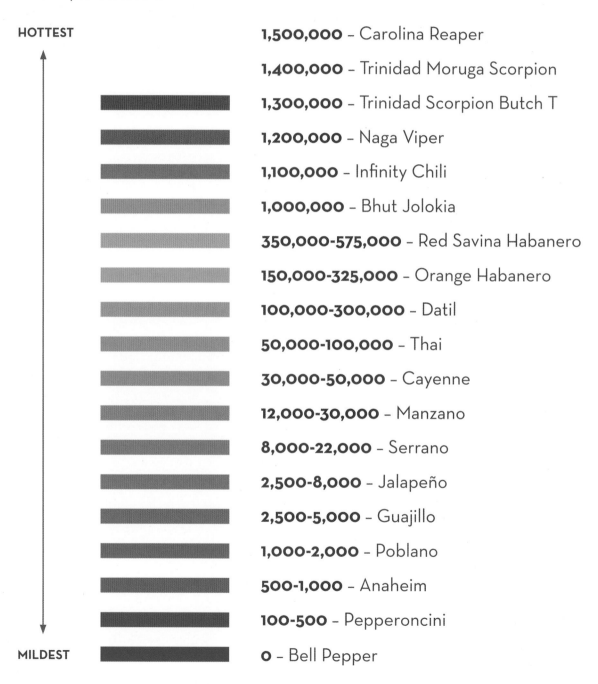

1,500,000 – Carolina Reaper

1,400,000 – Trinidad Moruga Scorpion

1,300,000 – Trinidad Scorpion Butch T

1,200,000 – Naga Viper

1,100,000 – Infinity Chili

1,000,000 – Bhut Jolokia

350,000-575,000 – Red Savina Habanero

150,000-325,000 – Orange Habanero

100,000-300,000 – Datil

50,000-100,000 – Thai

30,000-50,000 – Cayenne

12,000-30,000 – Manzano

8,000-22,000 – Serrano

2,500-8,000 – Jalapeño

2,500-5,000 – Guajillo

1,000-2,000 – Poblano

500-1,000 – Anaheim

100-500 – Pepperoncini

0 – Bell Pepper

MILDEST

Source: Alimentarium.com

ABOUT THE AUTHOR

Kim Thompson is a wife and mother of three amazing children. She is a down-to-earth, yet adventurous home cook, master organic gardener, photographer, artist, certified integrative nutrition health coach, student of naturopathy for over 17 years, and past contributor to Tend Magazine. Kim has studied various traditional and modern dietary theories and brings this knowledge along with her from the garden into her kitchen and medicinal pantry. She is always prepared with a well-stocked cupboard and freezer, preserving what she can and of course, saving her organic, home-grown seeds!

Growing up in an Italian, German, and English family, it was food that brought everyone together. Her path from the garden to the kitchen was a natural evolution throughout her life and nothing gives her greater joy than bringing smiles to the faces of family and friends with "homemade from the heart" fabulous food. She enjoys exploring all food cultures and the challenge of creatively juggling the dietary needs of the family. Time and again, Kim brings her zest for natural living to create inspiring dishes like those in Dandelions to Dinner, always incorporating any wild edibles and vegetables growing in her garden and yard.

Kim can be found on Instagram @organicgardengirl and online at organicgardengirl.com.